Into the Bible

101 routes to explore

Copyright SU 2007
First published 2007
ISBN 978 1 84427 274 7 (pack); 978 1 84427 295 2 (single)

Explanatory material and consultant: Mary Taylor
Lesson material written by: Kate Stevely
Lesson consultant: Gill Marchant

Scripture Union, 207–209 Queensway, Bletchley, Milton Keynes, MK2 2EB, UK.
Email: info@scriptureunion.org.uk
Website: www.scriptureunion.org.uk

Scripture Union Australia, Locked Bag 2, Central Coast Business Centre, NSW 2252.
Website: www.scriptureunion.org.au

British Library Cataloguing-in-Publication Data

A catalogue record of this book is available from the British Library.

Cover and internal design: David Lund
Illustration: David Mostyn
Internal layout: Creative Pages www.creativepages.co.uk

in association with Collins,
a division of HarperCollins Publishers, 77-85 Fulham Palace Road, London W6 8JB

Scriptures are taken from the Contemporary English version of the Bible, published by
Collins, part of HarperCollins Publishers © American Bible Society; Psalms © 1991,
1992; New Testament 1991,1992,1995; Old Testament 1995; Anglicisations © The
British and Foreign Bible Society 1997. For information on using text from the CEV, go
to www.biblesociety.org.uk/copyright

Printed and bound in Great Britain by Martins the Printers Ltd, Berwick upon Tweed

With thanks to Sarah Bell at St Margaret's CE Primary School, Bowers Gifford; Rev Cedd
Ambridge; William and Elizabeth Noad; Chris Luddington and Year 6 at Cassiobury Park
Junior School, Watford.

The letters BCE (Before the Common Era) and CE (Common Era) have been used in
preference to BC and AD because this is what is used in schools.

Scripture Union is an international Christian charity working with churches
in more than 130 countries, providing resources to bring the good news about Jesus
Christ to children, young people and families and to encourage them to develop
spiritually through the Bible and prayer.

As well as our network of volunteers, staff and associates who run holidays, church-
based events and school Christian groups, we produce a wide range of publications
and support those who use our resources through training programmes.

Into the Bible

story letter teaching poetry narrative prophecy
heroes villains travellers kings queens
romance shipwrecks miracles
Jews Greeks Romans
justice mercy
God

The Bible

101 routes Into the Bible to guide intrepid
explorers around and through the Bible!
Information, challenging questions,
inspirational people and 101 extracts from
the Bible itself!

Routemarkers – how *Into the Bible* works

 All 101 Routes into the Bible are numbered R – for example R45, R69. They are in the same order as you will find them in the Bible itself.

Maps

If you don't know where a place is, you look on a map. That's why there are maps in *Into the Bible*. You will be surprised to see the names of many places we know today.

Gecko notes!

This gecko or lizard gets everywhere. Of the many lizards in the Middle East, we like the name of the fan-foot lizard (*Ptyodactylus gecko*). It is reddish brown, spotted with white marks. The gecko lives on insects and worms, which it swallows whole. It gets its name 'gecko' from the peculiar sound it makes. You will find Gecko appearing on many pages in *Into the Bible*. How many times can you find him?

NSEW
This information will help you find your way around *Into the Bible*.

> **Verse 42:** In their thirteenth year, Jewish boys have a test of their knowledge of Scripture. They can then take their place as men in the Jewish community.

Verse box
Extra information to help make sense of a specific verse.

Arrows

One Route may lead to another one. These arrows help to make the right connections so you won't get lost. They will either direct you backwards or forwards – and sometimes in both directions. Sometimes what one writer wanted to say made sense to another writer 600 years later, so we have helped make the connections.

Inspirational people

Nine people, right at the centre of the Bible story, who could be described as especially inspirational. You can read about them on the IP pages. We could have included many others but you can't miss these nine!

Question

After each Route there is at least one question to make you think about what you have read.

Words in bold
At the back there is a glossary giving extra information on people, places and events. Any word **in bold** will be on this list!

Types of writing

The Bible is made up of different types of writing. Some of them overlap with each other. Seven types are used in *Into the Bible,* but we could have included names such as wisdom, apocalyptic, gospel, faith community stories and law.

 Old Testament This includes all the **Old Testament** extracts that tell the big story before Jesus came.

 Prophets Sometimes God sent messengers to tell his people and neighbouring nations how to live. These are mainly found in the Old Testament.

 Poetry God's people wrote and sang songs and poems, sometimes called psalms, to **worship** God or express their feelings. These are in the Old and New Testaments.

 New Testament This includes all the **New Testament** extracts that tell the big story about and after Jesus' birth.

 Story Lots of people in the Bible told stories or parables. The stories in *Into the Bible* are all ones told by Jesus.

 Teaching Jesus told people how God wanted them to live by teaching them – sometimes he used stories to do this.

 Letters Some **Christian** leaders wrote to the new followers of Jesus to help them live as God wants.

Routemarker facts

The **Old Testament** was mostly written in Hebrew. The **New Testament** was written in Greek.

The first translation of the Old and New Testaments, around the year 400CE, was in Latin which was the common language.

The expression 'Don't be afraid' appears 366 times in the Bible – one for every day of the year, even in a leap year.

From Abraham in the Old Testament to Paul in the New Testament is about 2000 years

The people of the Bible lived at the same time in history as the Egyptians, Greeks, Romans, Babylonians and Persians.

The first copies of the Bible were on rolls of papyrus (an old form of paper) or parchment (thin animal skin). Each book or section was on a separate scroll.

Routemarker facts

People who first translated the Bible into English knew that they could be imprisoned or put to death.

Nowadays Bibles can be downloaded onto hand-held computers or iPods.

The Bible is made up of 66 different books, written by many different authors.

About one third of the Old Testament books are prophecy, God's words about the present and the future. Many verses are quoted in the New Testament by Jesus and his followers.

Parts of the Bible have been translated into 2403 languages – 426 languages have a complete Bible, 1115 have a New Testament only and 862 have at least one book of the Bible. Work is still going on to translate the Bible into new languages.

In 1948 an Arab boy found some jars buried near the Dead Sea – they contained scrolls of the Bible text which date from around the time of Jesus.

How much of the Bible is in *Into the Bible*?

101 extracts from 27 Bible books have been chosen. They have been printed as you will find them in a full Bible, with chapters and verses. Here is how it works:

★ The Bible is divided up into 66 books. (The title of the book where you will find each extract is in the margin.)

★ Each book is divided into chapters. (Some books have fewer than five chapters. A few have over 40!)

★ Each chapter is divided into verses. (These are the small numbers in pale blue.)

★ Each verse is roughly one sentence.

Exodus 20:2

means the book of Exodus (the second book in the Bible), chapter 20, verse 2. You can find this in R20 page 52.

What is the Bible?

★ God's story

★ A book about God and people

★ God's rescue plan

★ Christians call it the Word of God

★ A collection of 66 books, with stories, poetry and writings by people inspired by God.

Some Bible books are very short – others cover many pages. Some of the books are stories about one person – like Jonah (R47). Some are about big events in world history, for example the destruction of Jerusalem – 2 Kings (R31). Every book of the Bible has a special place. They were collected together over hundreds of years.

What's the Bible for?

The writings in the Bible were recorded and collected to help people understand more about God, about living in God's way and about knowing God for themselves.

What's in the Bible?

The first major part of the Bible, the **Old Testament**, is the history of the way God related to one group of people, the **Jews**. (This part is also the Jewish holy book or Scriptures, known as the Tanakh.)

The second part, the **New Testament**, introduces Jesus, who he was, what he said and what he did. The Big Event in Jesus' life was his death on a cross, which led on to his resurrection, or coming alive again. The New Testament also tells the story of the first Christians and explains how Christians believe that anyone can enter a new relationship with God by trusting in what Jesus did. (The Jewish holy book does not have this part.)

A **Testament** is a legal agreement (like a last will and testament). In the Bible there are several agreements or covenants that God made with people. R56 explains more about the old and new agreements. The new agreement was not made by a set of laws, but by the life and death of Jesus himself.

What's the Bible's Big Story?

A rough story of the Bible (with a lot left out!). All the words in **bold** are in the glossary.

OLD TESTAMENT

God made the world → people disobey God → God sends a flood, only **Noah** and his family survive → God chooses **Abram** and **Sarai** to start his chosen people → they travel to Canaan → **Abraham**'s grandson **Jacob** (or **Israel**) takes large family to Egypt to escape famine → 400 years later they are slaves of the Egyptians → God sends **Moses** and rescues his people → travel through desert for 40 years → God gives ten commandments → God makes an agreement with the people → people settled in 'promised land' Canaan, led by Joshua → judges and then kings rule them → **David**, their second king, sets up capital in **Jerusalem** → David's son **Solomon** builds the temple → kings and people forget their agreement with God → God sends **prophets** to warn them → invading armies drive them out of their country → 70 years later they return, start to rebuild Jerusalem → God's people are waiting for the **Messiah**, a special messenger from God.

NEW TESTAMENT

An angel tells **Mary**, a young **Jewish** woman, 'You will have a son by the power of God's **Holy Spirit'** → **Joseph** marries his fiancée Mary and helps to bring the baby up → the baby is called Jesus → 30 years later, Jesus starts God's rescue plan → he makes people well, teaches them about 'God's **kingdom'** → he chooses 12 followers → people ask, 'Is this the **Messiah?'** → Jewish **priests** and leaders think that Jesus is committing blasphemy – showing disrespect to God → they arrest Jesus → they convince the Roman rulers that he is a threat → Romans kill Jesus on a wooden cross → friends bury Jesus in a **tomb** → two days later Jesus' body has gone → he has come back to life, and his followers see him → he explains why he had to die → 40 days later, Jesus leaves → God's **Holy Spirit** gives power to Jesus' followers → they spread the message of God's new agreement throughout the world → the **apostle Paul** travelled the most, through Turkey, Greece and Italy.

Where did it take place?

(See maps pages 27, 97, 121 and 183)

The Bible is set in the lands around the eastern end of the Mediterranean Sea. By the end of the Bible, Jesus' followers have travelled as far as Italy and Spain.

When did it take place?

★ Abraham's story takes place around 2000BCE – over 4000 years ago, in the Middle Bronze Age.

★ The estimated date of the birth of Jesus became the turning point in the Western calendar. Events before Jesus' birth are counted backwards and referred to as BCE (Before Common Era) or BC (Before Christ).

Events after Jesus' birth are counted forwards and referred to as CE (Common Era) or AD (Anno Domini, Latin for 'In the year of our Lord').

★ The events in the Bible end around 60 CE, though the last writer describes events in the future.

Who is in the Bible?

Find out in the Inspirational People pages (IP). Look for some of these characters…

What did the Bible look like?

The Old Testament was written in Hebrew and Aramaic (which looks like Hebrew). Specially trained writers (scribes) copied the text carefully onto long rolls of parchment, made of animal skins. The original Hebrew text looked something like this:

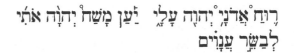

רוּחַ אֲדֹנָי יְהוִה עָלָי יַעַן מָשַׁח יְהוָה אֹתִי
לְבַשֵּׂר עֲנָוִים

These words are from Isaiah 61:1 (R42). Isaiah 61:1 in English looks like this:

> **The Spirit of the Lord God has taken control of me!**
> **The Lord has chosen and sent me to tell the**
> **oppressed the good news…**

When Jesus was asked to read the Scriptures in his home meeting place, he chose these same words from the prophet Isaiah (see Luke 4:18 – not in *Into the Bible*). In the New Testament, the words he spoke are written in Greek:

Πνεῦμα κυρίου ἐπ' ἐμέ, οὗ εἵνεκεν ἔχρισέν με
εὐαγγελίσασθαι πτωχοῖς,

What does the Bible look like now?

The Old Testament

Into the Bible contains extracts from 17 of the 39 books in the Old Testament, the ones written before the time of Jesus. It was hard to choose which extracts to include and there is far more left out than has been put in. After all, the Old Testament in a full Bible covers over 900 pages! But the stories, poems and prophecies in *Into the Bible* will give you the basic story of how God related to his people and how they responded.

You will meet most of the main characters who appear over many centuries of time.

You will travel from present-day Iraq to Israel, Egypt, Lebanon, Syria, Jordan and you will even encounter Jonah who headed off to Spain but never got there!

You will read of the promises God made to his people, all of which lead to part two of the Bible, the New Testament. You will have to turn to page 98 (R48) to start reading that.

You may choose to begin with R1 – the beginning. Or your eye might be caught by one of the Inspirational People – Abraham (IP1) or Jeremiah (IP5), or you may want to search for Gecko! Read wisely and enjoy.

R1

The beginning

Do you remember the day you were born? How do you know about it? What stories have you heard about it? The Bible begins with the birth of the world. That's what Genesis means – a beginning.

GENESIS 1:1 – 2:4

1 In the beginning God created the heavens and the earth. **2** The earth was barren, with no form of life; it was under a roaring ocean covered with darkness. But the **Spirit of God** was moving over the water.

The first day

3 God said, "I command light to shine!" And light started shining. **4** God looked at the light and saw that it was good. He separated light from darkness **5** and named the light "Day" and the darkness "Night". Evening came and then morning—that was the first day.

The second day

6 God said, "I command a dome to separate the water above it from the water below it."

7 And that's what happened. God made the dome **8** and named it "Sky". Evening came and then morning—that was the second day.

The third day

9 God said, "I command the water under the sky to come together in one place, so there will be dry

> **Verse 6** The writer gives a picture of an earth that was surrounded by water. The sky was like a 'dome' that came between the water on the earth (seas, lakes, rivers) and the water 'above the earth'.

ground." And that's what happened. **10** God named the dry ground "Land", and he named the water "Sea". God looked at what he had done and saw that it was good.

11 God said, "I command the earth to produce all kinds of plants, including fruit trees and grain." And that's what happened. **12** The earth produced all kinds of vegetation. God looked at what he had done, and it was good. **13** Evening came and then morning—that was the third day.

The fourth day

14 God said, "I command lights to appear in the sky and to separate day from night and to show the time for seasons, special days, and years. **15** I command them to shine on the earth." And that's what happened. **16** God made two powerful lights, the brighter one to rule the day and the other to rule the night. He also made the stars. **17** Then God put these lights in the sky to shine on the earth, **18** to rule day and night, and to separate light from darkness. God looked at what he had done, and it was good. **19** Evening came and then morning—that was the fourth day.

The fifth day

20 God said, "I command the sea to be full of living creatures, and I command birds to fly above the earth." **21** So God made the giant sea monsters and all the living creatures that swim in the sea. He also made every kind of bird. God looked at what he had done, and it was good. **22** Then he gave the living creatures his **blessing**—he told the sea creatures to live everywhere in the sea and the birds to live everywhere on earth. **23** Evening came and then morning—that was the fifth day.

The sixth day

24 God said, "I command the earth to give life to all kinds of tame animals, wild animals, and reptiles." And that's what happened. **25** God made every one of them. Then he looked at what he had done, and it was good.

26 God said, "Now we will make humans, and they will be like us. We will let them rule the fish, the birds, and all other living creatures."

27 So God created humans to be like himself; he made men and women. **28** God gave them his blessing and said:

Have a lot of children! Fill the earth with people and bring it under your control. Rule over the fish in the sea, the birds in the sky, and every animal on the earth.

29 I have provided all kinds of fruit and grain for you to eat. **30** And I have given the green plants as food for everything else that breathes. These will be food for animals, both wild and tame, and for birds"

31 God looked at what he had done. All of it was very good!

Evening came and then morning – that was the sixth day.

CHAPTER 2

1 So the heavens and the earth and everything else were created.

The seventh day

2 By the seventh day God had finished his work, and so he rested. **3** God **blessed** the seventh day and made it special because on that day he rested from his work.

4 That's how God created the heavens and the earth.

> **Q** What questions would you like to ask about the way the world began?

A deadly bite?

After the account of creation (pages 20–21), the Bible describes a beautiful garden, full of fruit trees and edible plants, in the area we now know as Iraq. Into this garden, God puts a man, many animals (not for food!), and finally a woman. The man and woman don't have names yet. There are two special trees – one gives life, one gives knowledge of right and wrong. God gives the man and woman two commands – DO look after the garden; DON'T eat the fruit from the tree of knowledge. It's a perfect world, until…

GENESIS 3:1–24

1 The snake was more cunning than any of the other wild animals that the LORD God had made. One day it came to the woman and asked, "Did God tell you not to eat fruit from any tree in the garden?"

2 The woman answered, "God said we could eat fruit from any tree in the garden, **3** except the one in the middle. He told us not to eat fruit from that tree or even to touch it. If we do, we will die."

4 "No, you won't!" the snake replied.

5 "God understands what will happen on the day you eat fruit from that tree. You will see what you have done, and you will know the difference between right and wrong, just as God does."

6 The woman stared at the fruit. It looked beautiful and tasty. She wanted the wisdom that it would give her, and she ate some of the fruit. Her husband was there with her, so she gave some to him, and he ate it too.

7 Straight away they saw what they had done, and they realized they were naked. Then they sewed fig leaves together to make something to cover themselves.

8 Late in the afternoon a breeze began to blow, and the man and woman heard the Lord God walking in the garden. They were frightened and hid behind some trees.

9 The Lord called out to the man and asked, "Where are you?"

10 The man answered, "I was naked, and when I heard you walking through the garden, I was frightened and hid!"

11 "How did you know you were naked?" God asked. "Did you eat any fruit from that tree in the middle of the garden?"

12 "It was the woman you put here with me," the man said. "She gave me some of the fruit, and I ate it."

13 The Lord God then asked the woman, "What have you done?"

"The snake tricked me," she answered. "And I ate some of that fruit."

14 So the Lord God said to the snake,

"Because of what you have done, you will be the only animal to suffer this curse—for as long as you live, you will crawl on your stomach and eat dust. **15** You and this woman will hate each other; your descendants and hers will always be enemies. One of hers will strike you on the head, and you will strike him on the heel."

16 Then the LORD said to the woman: "You will suffer terribly when you give birth. But you will still desire your husband, and he will rule over you."

17 The LORD said to the man:

"You listened to your wife and ate fruit from that tree. And so, the ground will be under a **curse** because of what you did. As long as you live, you will have to struggle to grow enough food.

18 Your food will be plants, but the ground will produce thorns and thistles. **19** You will have to sweat to earn a living; you were made out of soil, and you will once again turn into soil."

The man and woman chose not to live in the way that God planned. They chose to disobey God's instructions. The Bible calls this sin. The consequence or result of sin was being separated from God. Look for God's solutions to this problem in other parts of *Into the Bible*, for example R21, R56, R96.

20 The man **Adam** named his wife **Eve** because she would become the mother of all who live.

21 Then the LORD God made clothes out of animal skins for the man and his wife.

22 The LORD said, "These people now know the difference between right and wrong, just as we do. But they must not be allowed to eat fruit from the tree that lets them live for ever." **23** So the LORD God sent them out of the Garden of Eden, where they would have to work the ground from which the man had been made. **24** Then God put winged creatures at the entrance to the garden and a flaming, flashing sword to guard the way to the life-giving tree.

Q What's the most important thing to happen in this story? Why?

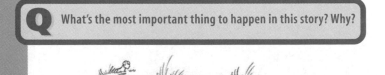

A new beginning

Many years pass, and God is no longer pleased with everything he has made (R1) because it ISN'T good – people have chosen to disobey God. All except one person. So God has a conversation with him…

GENESIS 6:13–18

13 So (God) told Noah:

"Cruelty and violence have spread everywhere. Now I'm going to destroy the whole earth and all its people. **14** Get some good timber and build a boat. Put rooms in it and cover it with tar inside and out. **15** Make it one hundred and thirty-three metres long, twenty-two metres wide, and thirteen metres high. **16** Build a roof on the boat and leave a space of about forty-four centimetres between the roof and the sides. Make the boat three storeys high and put a door on one side.

17 I'm going to send a flood that will destroy everything that breathes! Nothing will be left alive. **18** But I solemnly promise that you, your wife, your sons, and your daughters-in-law will be kept safe in the boat."

Noah did everything God told him to do.
The boat was longer than a football pitch, and was three storeys high.
Noah took seven pairs of some animals and birds, one pair of others.
God did everything that he said he'd do.
It rained, and the seas and rivers flooded.
The people and animals were on the boat for over a year! (Forty days of rain, five months for the water to go down, six months for the land to dry out.)

Promises, promises OT

After the earth has dried up and all the animals have left the boat, Noah and his family hear a special promise.

GENESIS 8:20–22

20 Noah built an **altar** where he could offer sacrifices to the LORD. Then he offered on the altar one of each kind of animal and bird that could be used for a **sacrifice**. **21** The smell of the burning offering pleased God, and he said:

> Never again will I punish the earth for the sinful things its people do. All of them have evil thoughts from the time they are young, but I will never destroy everything that breathes, as I did this time.
> **22** As long as the earth remains, there will be planting and harvest, cold and heat; winter and summer, day and night.

→

God's other covenants/ agreements R5, R19, R20, R45

GENESIS 9:8–13,17

8 Again, God said to Noah and his sons:

> **9** I am going to make a solemn promise to you and to everyone who will live after you. **10** This includes the birds and the animals that came out of the boat. **11** I promise every living creature that the earth and those living on it will never again be destroyed by a flood.
> **12–13** The rainbow that I have put in the sky will be my sign to you and to every living creature on earth. It will remind you that I will keep this promise for ever …
> **17** The rainbow will be the sign of that solemn promise.

> **Q** What was the sign that God would keep his promise? Think of a symbol to remind you of a promise you have made.

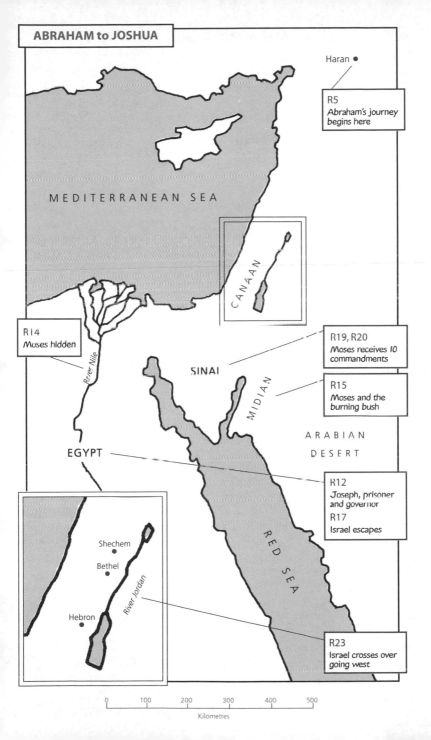

Abraham

⭐ Star factors

★ Believed and obeyed God
★ A man of faith

Key Bible verse

Abraham had faith and obeyed God. *Hebrews 11:8*

Big events in Abraham's life

Furthest	Travelled over 500km to a new country, because God told him to go (R5)
Bravest	Led 318 men to beat 4 armies, and won
Stupidest	Pretended his wife was his sister, to protect himself – twice
Most painful	Obeyed the command to be circumcised
Funniest	With Sarah, laughed when God told them they'd have a son because they were so very old. (A year later, Isaac was born – in Hebrew 'Isaac' sounds like 'laughs'.) (R8)
Hardest	see R8

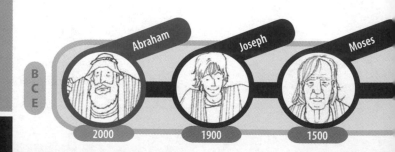

Abraham   Joseph   Moses

B C E

2000   1900   1500

What the Bible says about Abraham

★ He trusted God, again and again (R5, R6)

★ He built altars to show he had met God (R6)

★ He was given a name change by God, 'Abram' to 'Abraham' (means 'father of many nations')

★ He was seriously rich, owning sheep and cattle but no land, except a cave to bury Sarah

★ He didn't hear about God from his parents or friends but simply did what God told him to (R5)

And in the rest of the world in 2000BCE…

Only three of these would have been true in 2000BCE – which three are they?

A   Stonehenge has been built.
B   Chinese people are making silk.
C   Chinese people are making paper.
D   The Sphinx has been built.
E   The Greeks have invented the alphabet.

(answer below)

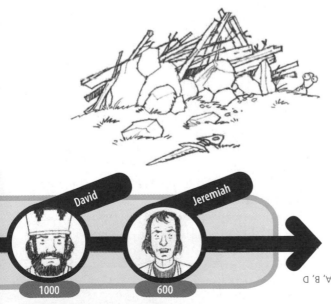

David

Jeremiah

1000

600

Into the unknown

Many years have passed since God's promises to Noah after the flood. People have settled in Canaan at the east end of the Mediterranean Sea, and God is ready for the next part of his action plan. But the person he has in mind lives about 450 miles away in Haran!

GENESIS 12:1–7

1 The LORD said to Abram:

Leave your country, your family, and your relatives and go to the land that I will show you. **2** I will **bless** you and make your **descendants** into a great nation. You will become famous and be a **blessing** to others. **3** I will bless anyone who blesses you, but I will put a **curse** on anyone who puts a curse on you. Everyone on earth will be blessed because of you.

4–5 Abram was seventy-five years old when the LORD told him to leave the city of Haran. He obeyed and left with his wife Sarai, his nephew Lot, and all the possessions and slaves they had got while in Haran.

When they came to the land of Canaan, **6** Abram went as far as the **sacred** tree of Moreh in a place called Shechem. The Canaanites were still living in the land at that time, **7** but the Lord appeared to Abram and promised, "I will give this land to your family for ever." Abram then built an **altar** there for the LORD.

Abram or Abraham – they're the same person! As part of their journey with God, Abram and Sarai were given new names – see page 33.

Q Abram is a big Bible hero. How would you feel if you were 75 and someone asked you to set off on a journey into the unknown?

The journey continues

Abram's journey continues, and he heads back to Canaan.

GENESIS 13:1–4, 14–18

1 Abram and Sarai took everything they owned and went to the Southern Desert. Lot went with them.

2 Abram was very rich. He owned many cattle, sheep, and goats, and had a lot of silver and gold. **3** Abram moved from place to place in the Southern Desert. And finally, he went north and set up his tents between Bethel and Ai, **4** where he had earlier camped and built an **altar**. There he **worshipped** the LORD.

The story continues…

Abram and his nephew Lot have so many animals that there isn't enough grazing land to feed them all. So Lot chooses to go to the Jordan Valley while Abram stays in Canaan.

14 After Abram and Lot had gone their separate ways, the LORD said to Abram:

Look around to the north, south, east, and west. **15** I will give you and your family all the land you can see. It will be theirs for ever! **16** I will give you more **descendants** than there are specks of dust on the earth, and some day it will be easier to count the specks of dust than to count your descendants. **17** Now walk back and forth across the land, because I am giving it to you.

18 Abram took down his tents and went to live near the sacred trees of Mamre at Hebron, where he built an **altar** in honour of the LORD.

> **Q** Abram built altars to mark that an important event had taken place in his **pilgrimage** of life. What do you do to mark important events in your life, or in the life of your community or school?

Different ways

God has promised Abram that he and Sarai will have a son, but after ten years the son still hasn't been born. Sarai knows the custom of that time – if her slave could have a child, the baby would count as Sarai's own. Life in Abram's time is very different from today – or is it?

GENESIS 16:1-16

1 Abram's wife Sarai had not been able to have any children. But she owned a young Egyptian slave woman named **Hagar**, **2** and Sarai said to Abram, "The LORD has not given me any children. Sleep with my slave, and if she has a child, it will be mine." Abram agreed, **3** and Sarai gave him Hagar to be his wife. This happened after Abram had lived in the land of Canaan for ten years. **4** Later, when Hagar knew she was going to have a baby, she became proud and was hateful to Sarai.

5 Then Sarai said to Abram, "It's all your fault! I gave you my slave woman, but she has been hateful to me ever since she found out she was pregnant. You have done me wrong, and you will have to answer to the LORD for this."

6 Abram said, "All right! She's your slave, and you can do whatever you want with her." But Sarai began treating Hagar so harshly that she finally ran away.

7 Hagar stopped to rest at a spring in the desert on the road to Shur. While she was there, the **angel** of the LORD came to her **8** and asked, "Hagar, where have you come from, and where are you going?" She answered, "I'm running away from Sarai, my owner."

9 The angel said, "Go back to Sarai and be her slave. **10–11** I will give you a son, who will be called **Ishmael**, because I have heard your cry for help. And later I will give you so

many descendants that no one will be able to count them all.
12 But your son will live far from his relatives; he will be like a wild donkey, fighting everyone, and everyone fighting him."

13 Hagar thought, "Have I really seen God and lived to tell about it?" So from then on she called him, "The God who Sees Me". **14** That's why people call the well between Kadesh and Bered, "The Well of the Living One who Sees Me".

15-16 Abram was eighty-six years old when Hagar gave birth to their son, and he named him **Ishmael**.

→

R15

> **Q** How did Hagar mark her meeting with God?

> **Q** Have you ever tried hard to get something you wanted – but found it wasn't what you expected? What did you do then?

The test

R8

Genesis 22:1–14

Thirteen years have passed since Ishmael was born. God has given new names to Abraham (meaning father of many nations) and Sarah (meaning princess). God promises that Sarah will have a son, and a year later Isaac is born. God has kept his promise and Abraham is still following God.

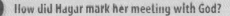

GENESIS 22:1–14

1 Some years later God decided to test Abraham, so he spoke to him.

Abraham answered, "Here I am, LORD."

2 The Lord said, "Go and get Isaac, your only son, the one you dearly love! Take him to the land of Moriah, and I will show you a mountain where you must sacrifice him to me on the fires of an **altar**." **3** So Abraham got up early the next morning and chopped wood for the fire. He put a saddle on his donkey and left with Isaac and two servants for the place where God had told him to go.

Scary times... the custom for some tribes in the land of Canaan was to kill children as part of a **worship** ceremony (a **sacrifice**). Would God want Abraham to act like this too?

4 Three days later Abraham looked into the distance and saw the place. **5** He told his servants, "Stay here with the donkey, while my son and I go over there to worship. We will come back."

6 Abraham put the wood on Isaac's shoulder, but he carried the hot coals and the knife. As the two of them walked along, **7–8** Isaac said, "Father, we have the coals and the wood, but where is the lamb for the sacrifice?"

"My son," Abraham answered, "God will provide the lamb."

The two of them walked on, and

9 when they reached the place that God had told him about, Abraham built an altar and placed the wood on it. Next, he tied up his son and put him on the wood. **10** He then took the knife and got ready to kill his son. **11** But the LORD's angel shouted from heaven, "Abraham! Abraham!"

"Here I am!" he answered.

12 "Don't hurt the boy or harm him in any way!" the angel said. "Now I know that you truly obey God, because you were willing to offer him your only son."

Abraham's experience on Mount Moriah is important for Jews, Christians and Muslims but they may interpret it differently.

13 Abraham looked up and saw a ram caught by its horns in the bushes.

So he took the ram and sacrificed it in place of his son.

14 Abraham named that place "The LORD will Provide". And even now people say, "On the mountain of the LORD it will be provided."

> **Q** The writer ended with a common saying about these events. What do you want to say about what happened on the mountain?

Jacob's dream

About ninety years have passed. Abraham's son Isaac marries Rebekah (his cousin, who comes from Haran) and has twin sons, Esau and Jacob. Although Jacob is the younger twin, he tricks his father Isaac into getting the rights that are due to Esau, the firstborn. Now Esau has found out and wants to kill his brother. Jacob runs to his relatives in Haran – about 720 km away.

GENESIS 28:10–17

10 Jacob left the town of Beersheba and started out for Haran. **11** At sunset he stopped for the night and went to sleep, resting his head on a large rock. **12** In a dream he saw a ladder that reached from earth to **heaven**, and God's **angels** were going up and down on it.
13 The LORD was standing beside the ladder and said:

After this encounter, Jacob calls the place Beth-el, which means 'house of God'.

I am the LORD God who was worshipped by Abraham and Isaac. I will give to you and your family the land on which you are now sleeping. **14** Your **descendants** will spread over the earth in all directions and will become as numerous as the specks of dust. Your family will be a blessing to all people. **15** Wherever you go, I will watch over you, then later I will bring you back to this land. I won't leave you—I will do all I have promised.

16 Jacob woke up suddenly and thought, "The LORD is in this place, and I didn't even know it." **17** Then Jacob became frightened and said, "This is a fearsome place! It must be the house of God and the ladder to heaven."

> **Q** Jacob remembered this dream for the rest of his life. Later, he came back to Bethel to thank God. Do you remember any of your dreams?

R10 A meeting at night [OT]

Jacob reaches his uncle, falls in love with Laban's younger daughter and works as a shepherd for seven years so he can marry her. But Laban tricks him into marrying his older daughter Leah! He marries Rachel too – but works for another seven years... and is tricked into another six years' work to earn the sheep and goats that are born while he is looking after the flock. Jacob plays the final trick and leaves with his wives, children and many animals.

GENESIS 32:22–30

22–23 Jacob got up in the middle of the night and took his wives, his eleven children, and everything he owned across to the other side of the River Jabbok for safety. **24** Afterwards, Jacob went back and spent the rest of the night alone.

A man came and fought with Jacob until just before daybreak. **25** When the man saw that he could not win, he struck Jacob on the hip and threw it out of joint. **26** They kept on wrestling until the man said, "Let go of me! It's almost daylight."

"You can't go until you **bless** me," Jacob replied.

27 Then the man asked, "What is your name?"

"Jacob," he answered.

28 The man said, "Your name will no longer be Jacob. You have wrestled with God and with men, and you have won. That's why your name will be Israel."

29 Jacob said, "Now tell me your name."

"Don't you know who I am?" he asked. And he blessed Jacob.

30 Jacob said, "I have seen God face to face, and I am still alive." So he named the place Peniel.

At that time a man could be married to more than one wife at a time. Jacob had four wives – Rachel, Leah and their servants Bilhah and Zilpah.

Q Did you guess who Jacob was wrestling with? If you did, what were the clues?

My family

Jacob (now known as Israel) has settled back in Canaan with his wives Leah, Bilhah and Zilpah, his daughter and his twelve sons. His best-loved wife, Rachel, has died giving birth to her second son Benjamin. Her first son, Joseph, is his father's favourite.

GENESIS 37:1–11,17–28,36

1 Jacob lived in the land of Canaan, where his father Isaac had lived, **2** and this is the story of his family.

When Jacob's son Joseph was seventeen years old, he took care of the sheep with his brothers, the sons of Bilhah and Zilpah. But he was always telling his father all sorts of bad things about his brothers.

3 Jacob loved Joseph more than he did any of his other sons, because Joseph was born after Jacob was very old. Jacob had given Joseph a fine coat **4** to show that he was his favourite son, and so Joseph's brothers hated him and would not be friendly to him.

5 One day, Joseph told his brothers what he had dreamed, and they hated him even more. **6** Joseph said, "Let me tell you about my dream. **7** We were out in the field, tying up bundles of wheat. Suddenly my bundle stood up, and your bundles gathered around and bowed down to it."

8 His brothers asked, "Do you really think you are going to be king and rule over us?" Now they hated Joseph more than ever because of what he had said about his dream.

9 Joseph later had another dream, and he told his brothers, "Listen to what else I dreamed. The sun, the moon, and eleven stars bowed down to me."

10 When he told his father about this dream, his father became angry and said, "What's that supposed to mean? Are your mother and I and your brothers all going to come and bow down in front of you?"

11 Joseph's brothers were jealous of him, but his father kept wondering about the dream.

The story continues...

Jacob sends Joseph to find his brothers who are out with the sheep, a long way from home. His brothers see him coming...

17 Joseph … found his brothers in Dothan. **18** But before he got there, they saw him coming and made plans to kill him. **19** They said to one another, "Look, here comes the hero of those dreams! **20** Let's kill him and throw him into a pit and say that some wild animal ate him. Then we'll see what happens to those dreams."

21 Reuben heard this and tried to protect Joseph from them. "Let's not kill him," he said. **22** "Don't murder him or even harm him. Just throw him into a dry well out here in the desert." Reuben planned to rescue Joseph later and take him back to his father.

The story continues…

After Reuben has gone, they throw Joseph into the well, sit down for lunch and see a group of Midianite traders coming by on their camels.

26 So Judah said, "What will we gain if we kill our brother and hide his body? **27** Let's sell him to the Ishmaelites and not harm him. After all, he is our brother." And the others agreed.

28 When the Midianite merchants came by, Joseph's brothers took him out of the well, and for twenty pieces of silver they sold him to the Ishmaelites who took him to Egypt

> **Verse 28** the merchants came from an area between Egypt and Canaan.

… 36 Meanwhile, the Midianites had sold Joseph in Egypt to a man named **Potiphar**, who was the king's official in charge of the palace guard.

The story continues…

Reuben returns and realises he is too late to save Joseph. The brothers tear Joseph's coat, put goat's blood on it and pretend to their father that Joseph has been killed by wild animals. Jacob is heartbroken.

> **Q** Can you imagine how Joseph, his brothers and his father felt?

R12 · Any dream will do? OT

There are not enough pages in *Into the Bible* to include all the exciting Joseph story but you can read it in Genesis chapters 39 to 49. Instead, here's Joseph's story in 179 words! Look out for the dreams, the cows and the silver cup...

Joseph works hard for Potiphar, but Potiphar's wife has Joseph arrested → Joseph works hard in prison → explains dreams of king's two servants → one servant released but forgets Joseph in prison.

Two years later, king has frightening dreams → for example, seven thin cows eat seven fat cows → king's advisers can't explain. Servant remembers Joseph → Joseph released, says God can explain dreams → seven years of famine will follow seven good years.

Joseph becomes governor → organises food storage → famine comes → ten of Joseph's brothers come for food → don't recognise 'Egyptian' brother → Joseph tests them → accuses them of spying, lets nine go but must return with youngest brother **Benjamin**.

Jacob (dad) won't let Ben go → famine gets worse → brothers take Ben to Egypt → Joseph sets trap → Benjamin has stolen silver cup! → **Judah** offers to go to prison in place of Benjamin.

Joseph knows brothers have changed → tells brothers who he is → great reunion → brothers bring Jacob and family (70 people) from Canaan → God makes promise to Jacob that his descendants will return → Jacob meets Joseph again → family given the best land in Egypt.

For the best

GENESIS 50:15–21

The story continues...

15 After Jacob died, Joseph's brothers said to each other, "What if Joseph still hates us and wants to get even with us for all the cruel things we did to him?"
16 So they sent this message to Joseph:

Before our father died, **17** he told us, "You did some cruel and terrible things to Joseph, but you must ask him to forgive you."

Now we ask you to forgive the terrible things we did. After all, we serve the same God that your father worshipped. When Joseph heard this, he started crying.
18 At once, Joseph's brothers came and bowed down to the ground in front of him and said, "We are your slaves."
19 But Joseph told them, "Don't be afraid! I have no right to change what God has decided. **20** You tried to harm me, but God made it turn out for the best, so that he could save all these people, as he is now doing.
21 Don't be afraid! I will take care of you and your children." After Joseph said this, his brothers felt much better.

Q Which part of the story of Joseph and his brothers did you like best?

Q What would you say was Joseph's destiny?

Joseph

⭐ Star factor

★ **Kept working until God changed things**

What Joseph says about God

"I can't do it myself, but God can…" *Genesis 41:16*

Key Bible verse

"You tried to harm me, but God made it turn out for the best, so that he could save all these people, as he is now doing." *Genesis 50:20* (R13)

Big events in Joseph's life

Dreamiest	Had dreams and explained them to his brothers – who hated him (R11)
Saddest	Brothers planned to kill him, but sold him instead (R11)
Most unfair	Had good job in Egypt but falsely accused of wrongdoing and sent to prison (R12)
Most powerful	Governor of Egypt – saved grain during good years (R12)
Happiest	Arranged reunion with brothers and father (R13)

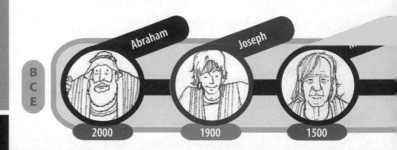

Abraham   Joseph

B C E

2000   1900   1500

What the Bible says about Joseph

★ His family had 1 father, 4 mothers, 12 sons and 1 daughter

★ He was the favourite son (R11)

★ Wherever Joseph worked, things went well for his employer (R12)

★ He and his Egyptian wife had two sons who had names to remind him of his family

★ When he cried, everyone heard him

And in the rest of Egypt in 1900BCE...

The Pyramids and the Sphinx were already 1000 years old!

Egyptian pharaohs were still building on a grand scale.

Egyptians were already writing hieroglyphs on stone (which can still be seen) and papyrus (which can't).

Egyptians believed in gods based on things they could see – the sun, moon, the river Nile.

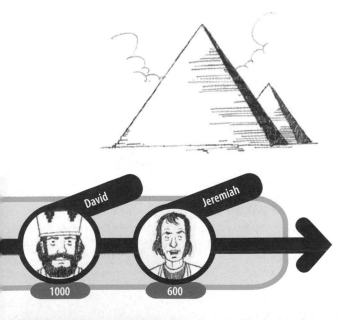

David

Jeremiah

1000   600

Water baby

If you were travelling in Greece, you'd see the word Exodus on a lot of road signs! It means exit, or the way out and it's a big clue to what the second book of the Bible is about.

The story so far...

About 400 years have passed since Jacob (Israel) and his family moved to Egypt when Jacob's son Joseph saved Egypt from famine. The new Pharaoh or king of Egypt has forgotten about Joseph. Jacob's descendants, the **Israelites** (or **Hebrews**), are now Egyptian slaves. The king has given orders for baby Hebrew boys to be killed at birth, but the midwives save their lives. He then orders his soldiers to throw all baby boys into the river Nile.

EXODUS 2:1–10

1 A man from the Levi tribe married a woman from the same tribe, **2** and she later had a baby boy. He was a beautiful child, and she kept him inside for three months. **3** But when she could no longer keep him hidden, she made a basket out of reeds and covered it with tar. She put him in the basket and placed it in the tall grass along the edge of the River Nile. **4** The baby's elder sister stood at a distance to see what would happen to him.

5 About that time one of the king's daughters came down to take a bath in the river, while her servant women walked along the river bank. She saw the basket in the tall grass and sent one of the young women to pull it out of the water. **6** When the king's daughter opened the basket, she saw the baby and felt sorry for him because he was crying. She said, "This must be one of the Hebrew babies."

7 At once the baby's elder sister came up and asked, "Do you want me to get a Hebrew woman to take care of the baby for you?"

8 "Yes," the king's daughter answered.

So the girl brought the baby's mother, **9** and the king's daughter told her, "Take care of this child, and I will pay you." The baby's mother carried him home and took care of him.

10 And when he was old enough, she took him to the king's daughter, who adopted him. She named him Moses because she said, "I pulled him out of the water."

> **Q** Moses was well looked after! His older sister, his birth mum, the mum who adopted him – they all played a part in keeping Moses safe. Think about the people who look after you.

Fiery words

Although Moses is adopted by the king's daughter and brought up as a prince, he remembers his Israelite background and his ancestors *Abraham*, *Isaac* and *Jacob* who trusted God. One day Moses kills an Egyptian who is mistreating an Israelite. He runs to the desert area of Midian (see map page 27), where he works for 40 years as a shepherd. Meanwhile the Israelite slaves are still suffering and crying to God for help.

EXODUS 3:1–12,14–15

1 One day, Moses was taking care of the sheep and goats of his father-in-law Jethro, the **priest** of Midian, and Moses decided to lead them across the desert to Sinai, the **holy**

mountain. **2** There an **angel** of the L ORD appeared to him from a burning bush. Moses saw that the bush was on fire, but it was not burning up. **3** "This is strange!" he said to himself. "I'll go over and see why the bush isn't burning up." **4** When the L ORD saw Moses coming near the bush, he called him by name, and Moses answered, "Here I am." **5** God replied, "Don't come any closer. Take off your sandals—the ground where you are standing is holy. **6** I am the God who was **worshipped** by your ancestors Abraham, Isaac, and Jacob."

Moses was afraid to look at God, and so he hid his face. **7** The L ORD said:

I have seen how my people are suffering as slaves in Egypt, and I have heard them beg for my help because of the way they are being ill-treated. I feel sorry for them, **8** and I have come down to rescue them from the Egyptians.

> **Verse 8** All these tribes lived in the land that God had promised to give Abraham (see R6 and R23).

I will bring my people out of Egypt into a country where there is good land, rich with milk and honey. I will give them the land where the Canaanites, Hittites, Amorites, Perizzites, Hivites, and Jebusites now live. **9** My people have begged for my help, and I have seen how cruel the Egyptians are to them. **10** Now go to the king! I am sending you to lead my people out of his country.

11 But Moses said, "Who am I to go to the king and lead your people out of Egypt?"
12 God replied, "I will be with you. And you will know that I am the one who sent you, when you worship me on this mountain after you have led my people out of Egypt…

14–15 I am the eternal God. So tell them that the L ORD, whose

Names of God
I am: When God speaks to Moses, he uses a special name to describe himself which we can't translate into English – I am the one who has always been and will always be. In Hebrew it is shown by four consonants, YHWH, but is never spoken. Jewish people often used the word 'Adonai, which is usually translated as 'the L ORD' in capital letters.

R7

name is "I Am", has sent you. this is my name for ever and it is the name that people must use from now on."

> **Q** Where do people go to meet God now?

> **Q** How does God get Moses' attention? If you were God, how would you get people's attention so you could speak to them?

Let my people go

R16

God gives Moses a job – to speak to the king of Egypt. Moses isn't sure he wants the job. So God shows Moses signs of his power. Moses still isn't sure! God agrees for Moses to go with his older brother Aaron, who's a great talker. Moses accepts, meets Aaron and speaks to the Israelites.

EXODUS 5:1–2

1 Moses and Aaron went to the king of Egypt and told him, "The LORD God says, 'Let my people go into the desert, so they can honour me with a celebration there.'"
2 "Who is this LORD and why should I obey him?" the king replied. "I refuse to let you and your people go!"

The story continues…

To put pressure on the king, God sends nine disasters (or plagues) on the people of Egypt – see page 48 and 49. The king still refuses. After the ninth disaster, Moses warns that he won't come back. God gives Moses detailed instructions to prepare the Israelites for the final disaster, but Moses never returns to the king's palace. The king has had his final warning.

> **Q** Why do you think the king refused to let the people go?

R17 Go!

OT

Imagine the happiest day of your life mixed with the saddest time you've ever had – and you'll have some idea of the night of the Exodus or exit from Egypt. The Israelite people hear of the terrible disaster that is coming to Egypt – and the only way to save themselves is to follow God's instructions for a special meal. Their lives will be saved by the blood of the sheep that they eat at the Passover feast.

EXODUS 12:21–25,29–34,37,40–42

21 Moses called the leaders of Israel together and said:

Each family is to pick out a sheep and kill it for Passover. **22** Make a brush from a few small branches of a hyssop plant and dip the brush in the bowl that has the blood of the animal in it. Then brush some of the blood above the door and on the posts at each side of the door of your house. After this, everyone is to stay inside.

23 During that night the LORD will go through the country of Egypt and kill the firstborn son in every Egyptian family. He will see where you have put the blood, and he will not come into your house. His **angel** that brings death will pass over and not kill your firstborn sons.

24–25 After you have entered the country promised to

you by the LORD, you and your children must continue to celebrate **Passover** each year.

29 At midnight the LORD killed the firstborn son of every Egyptian family, from the son of the king to the son of every prisoner in jail. He also killed the firstborn male of every animal that belonged to the Egyptians.

30 That night the king, his officials, and everyone else in Egypt got up and started crying bitterly. In every Egyptian home, someone was dead.

31 During the night the king sent for Moses and Aaron and told them, "Get your people out of my country and leave us alone! Go and **worship** the LORD, as you have asked. **32** Take your sheep, goats, and cattle, and get out. But ask your God to be kind to me."

33 The Egyptians did everything they could to get the Israelites to leave their country fast. They said, "Please hurry and leave. If you don't, we will all be dead." **34** So the Israelites quickly made some bread dough and put it in pans. But they did not mix any yeast in the dough to make it rise.

40–41 The LORD's people left Egypt exactly four hundred and thirty years after they had arrived. On that night the LORD kept watch for them, and on this same night each year Israel will always keep watch in honour of the LORD.

> **Verse 42** Jewish families still keep Moses' command and hold the Passover feast every year, in March or April. They eat a roast meal and bread without yeast, to remember that they left in a hurry with no time to let the bread rise.

> **Q** The Israelites were free at last. The Egyptians were devastated. Think about the cost to the Israelites of their freedom.

R18 Cross over

Thousands of Israelite children and adults leave Egypt, plus animals. God has rescued them from being slaves, and is leading them to a new country. They have to trust God and their leader, Moses. God shows he is with them by a cloud which goes ahead during the day and a tall pillar of fire at night. They head for the Red Sea (or Sea of Reeds) and then they realize that the Egyptian king has broken his promise again, and is following them. Soldiers behind and water ahead. Where can they go?

EXODUS 14:21–29

21 Moses stretched his arm over the sea, and the LORD sent a strong east wind that blew all night until there was dry land where the water had been. The sea opened up, **22** and the Israelites walked through on dry land with a wall of water on each side.

23 The Egyptian chariots and cavalry went after them. **24** But before daylight the LORD looked down at the Egyptian army from the fiery cloud and made them panic. **25** Their chariot wheels got stuck, and it was hard for them to move. So the Egyptians said to one another, "Let's leave these people alone! The LORD is on their side and is fighting against us."

26 The LORD told Moses, "Stretch your arm towards the sea—the water will cover the Egyptians and their cavalry and chariots." **27** Moses stretched out his arm, and at daybreak the water rushed towards the Egyptians. They tried to run away, but the LORD drowned them in the sea. **28** The water came and covered the chariots, the cavalry, and the whole Egyptian army that had followed the Israelites into the sea. Not one of them was left alive. **29** But the sea had made a wall of water on each side of the Israelites; so they walked through on dry land.

Q The Israelites believe that God has saved them again. What would you say to someone who saved your life?

Do you agree?

R19

Exodus 19:3–8,16–20

R4, R6

The Israelites have arrived at Mount Sinai in the desert. They know that God has rescued them. Now they need to find out why. God has already made agreements with Noah (R4) and Abraham (R6). Now he is about to make a covenant or agreement with all the Israelites.

EXODUS 19:3–8,16–20

3 Moses went up the mountain to meet with the LORD God, who told him to say to the people:

4 You saw what I did in Egypt, and you know how I brought you here to me, just as a mighty eagle carries its young. **5** Now if you will faithfully obey me, you will be my very own people. The whole world is mine, **6** but you will be my **holy** nation and serve me as **priests**.

Moses, that is what you must tell the Israelites.

Covenants or agreements or treaties
At the time of Moses, countries or tribes would often make covenants or treaties with each other. Each side would draw up a list of conditions, which they agreed to do in order to respect the covenant.

7 After Moses went back, he reported to the leaders what the LORD had said, **8** and they promised, "We will do everything the LORD has commanded." So Moses told the LORD about this.
16 On the morning of the third day, there was thunder and

51

lightning. A thick cloud covered the mountain, a loud trumpet blast was heard and everyone in camp trembled with fear. **17** Moses led them out of the camp to meet God and they stood at the foot of the mountain.

18 Mount Sinai was covered with smoke because the LORD has come down in a flaming fire. Smoke poured out of the mountain just like a furnace and the whole mountain shook. **19** The trumpet blew louder and louder. Moses spoke and God answered him with thunder.

20 The LORD came down to the top of Mount Sinai and told Moses to meet him there.

> **Q** Think about any agreements you have made. Are you both keeping to your side of the agreement? Is there something you need to do to make the agreement work better?

R20

Ten Commandments

The setting is the same – the Israelites are in the desert around Mount Sinai. God has appeared in thunder and lightning above the mountain. Moses goes up the mountain to hear more about the treaty or covenant that God is making with the people.

R21

EXODUS 20:1–17

1 God said to the people of Israel:

2 I am the LORD your God, the one who brought you out of Egypt where you were slaves.
3 Do not **worship** any god except me.
4 Do not make **idols** that look like anything in the sky or on earth or in the sea under the earth. **5** Don't bow down

and worship idols. I am the LORD your God, and I demand all your love. If you reject me, I will punish your families for three or four generations. **6** But if you love me and obey my laws, I will be kind to your families for thousands of generations.

7 Do not misuse my name. I am the LORD your God, and I will punish anyone who misuses my name.

8 Remember that the **Sabbath Day** belongs to me. **9** You have six days when you can do your work, **10** but the seventh day of each week belongs to me, your God. No one is to work on that day—not you, your children, your slaves, your animals, or the foreigners who live in your towns. **11** In six days I made the sky, the earth, the seas, and everything in them, but on the seventh day I rested. That's why I made the Sabbath a special day that belongs to me.

← R1 God rests

12 Respect your father and your mother, and you will live a long time in the land I am giving you.

13 Do not murder.

14 Be faithful in marriage.

15 Do not steal.

16 Do not tell lies about others.

17 Do not want to take anything that belongs to someone else. Don't want to take anyone's house, wife or husband, slaves, oxen, donkeys or anything else.

Q Which command do you think is the hardest one to follow?

Moses

⭐ Star factor

★ Led people and showed them what God was like

Key Bible verse

There has never again been a prophet in Israel like Moses. The LORD spoke face to face with him...
Deuteronomy 34:10

Big events in Moses' life

Boldest	Ordered King of Egypt to let the Israelites leave Egypt (R16)
Bravest	Led Israelites out of Egypt and through the Red Sea (R18)
Most amazing	Met God at Mount Sinai and heard God's **commandments** (R19, R20)
Toughest	Led Israelites around the desert for 40 years
Most disappointing	Saw new country before he died, but never entered it

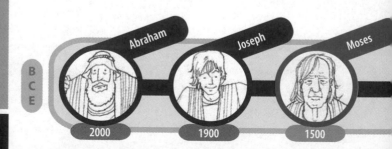

BCE

Abraham — 2000

Joseph — 1900

Moses — 1500

What the Bible says about Moses

★ He was adopted when he was a baby (R14)

★ He had an older brother and sister – he met them when he was older (R14)

★ He thought he wasn't a good speaker (R15)

★ He was 80 when he started his new job

★ He talked to God about everything

★ He got angry when people broke their promise to God.

Law and Order, 1500 BCE

Around the same time as Moses, Hammurabi, king of Assyria, made laws (282 of them) which were written on a stone nearly 3m high! A copy of Hammurabi's Stele (rock) can still be seen in the Louvre museum in Paris, but his laws are no longer followed.

The Ten Commandments were given by God and also written on stone. The stones have been lost, but the laws survive in the pages of the Old Testament – and in the legal code of many countries.

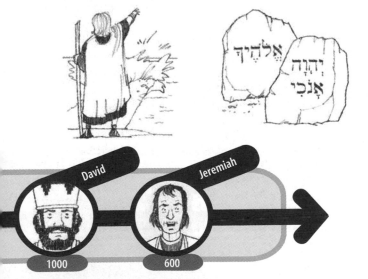

David

Jeremiah

1000

600

R19, R20

R56
R59
R86

Take it away

After Genesis, the opening books of the Bible have a lot of detail of how the Israelites are going to worship God. This is especially so with the third book, Leviticus. There are instructions about how they eat, what they wear and what they do when they meet at God's special place. Jewish people still keep many of these laws. The most important thing was for the people to remember that God is holy, separate from them. The

people still tended to do the wrong thing and let God down. So God had to give them a way to say sorry, and to make it possible for their sins or wrong things to be taken away. This was how it happened under the first covenant or agreement he made with his people (R19). It all changed with the death of Jesus (R59).

LEVITICUS 16:20–22

20 After you have purified the most holy place, the sacred tent, and the bronze altar, you must bring the live goat to the front of the tent. **21** There you will lay your hands on its head, while confessing every sin the people have committed, and you will appoint someone to lead the goat into the desert, so that it can take away their sins. **22** Finally, this goat that carries the heavy burden of Israel's sins must be released deep in the desert.

Q This goat became known as the scapegoat. People still use this word when they talk about someone who takes all the blame, even if they didn't do anything. Has this ever happened to you? Or has someone taken the blame for something you did?

One commandment

This Bible book with a long name means 'repeat the law'. In this book, Moses repeats many of the laws from Exodus and Leviticus, before the people cross into their new country. (Look at the map on page 27 to see where they had to go.) Moses also finds different ways of telling people about God's commands, so that they will remember them after Moses has gone.

DEUTERONOMY 6:1–9

Moses said to Israel:

1 The LORD told me to give you these laws and teachings, so you can obey them in the land he is giving you. Soon you will cross the River Jordan and take that land. **2** And if you and your descendants want to live a long time, you must always **worship** the LORD and obey his laws. **3** Pay attention, Israel! Our ancestors worshipped the LORD, and he promised to give us this land that is rich with milk and honey. Be careful to obey him, and you will become a successful and powerful nation.

4 Listen, Israel! The LORD our God is the only true God! **5** So love the LORD your God with all your heart, soul, and strength. **6** Memorize his **laws 7** and tell them to your children over and over again. Talk about them all the time, whether you're at home or walking along the road or going to bed at night, or getting up in the morning. **8** Write down copies and tie them to your wrists and foreheads to help you obey them. **9** Write these laws on the door frames of your homes and on your town gates.

> **Verses 4–5** This command is known by Jews as the Shema or great commandment. It summarises the **Ten Commandments** (R20).

> **Q** Moses gave the people lots of ways to remember God's laws. What helps you to remember things that are important to you?

R23 A new leader

Moses has died. He has led thousands of Israelite **children and animals, women and men to the border of the new country that God promised them. Now they have a new leader, Joshua. They also have their first big challenge – a river between them and the new land – and not a bridge, tunnel or boat in sight…**

JOSHUA 3:1,9–10,14–17

1 Early the next morning, Joshua and the Israelites packed up and left Acacia. They went to the River Jordan and camped there that night.

9 Joshua spoke to the people:

Come here and listen to what the LORD our God said he will do!
10 The Canaanites, the Hittites, the Hivites, the Perizzites, the Girgashites, the Amorites, and the Jebusites control the land on the other side of the river. But the living God will be with you and will force them out of the land when you attack. And now, God is going to prove that he's powerful enough to force them out…

> **Verse 10** These are the tribes who live in this new country. They are fierce fighters and have well-guarded towns. They follow other gods and don't follow the God of Israel.

14 The Israelites packed up and left camp. The **priests** carrying **the (sacred) chest** walked in front, **15** until they came to the River Jordan. The water in the river had risen over its banks, as it often does in springtime. But as soon as the feet of the priests touched the water, **16–17** the river stopped flowing, and the water started piling up at the town of Adam near Zarethan. No water flowed towards the Dead Sea, and the priests stood in the middle of the dry river bed near Jericho while everyone else crossed over.

R18

Joshua is a Hebrew name which means 'God saves'. The Greek name for Joshua is Jesus.

The story continues…

Joshua leads the people into Canaan. They fight many battles but do not drive the other tribes out, as God had commanded. But before Joshua dies, the Israelites promise to serve God.

> **Q** The people crossing the river Jordan at this time would have been children when they left Egypt. What memories might have come flooding back when the river stopped flowing?

I'll stand by you

R24

During the time of the judges, who led the people after Joshua, there is a famine. Naomi, Elimelech and their two sons move from Bethlehem to the country of Moab. The sons marry girls from Moab. But Elimelech and his sons die, leaving Naomi with her daughters-in-law Ruth and Orpah. Naomi decides to return to her home country of Judah. Her two daughters-in-law go with her but Orpah turns back. Ruth, however, makes this moving promise of commitment to her mother-in-law.

RUTH 1:16–18

16 Ruth answered,

"Please don't tell me to leave you and return home! I will go where you go,
I will live where you live; your people will be my people, your God will be my God.
17 I will die where you die and be buried beside you.
May the LORD punish me if we are ever separated, even by death!"

18 When Naomi saw that Ruth had made up her mind to go with her, she stopped urging her to go back.

The story continues...

Naomi arrives back in her home town, Bethlehem. Ruth helps by gathering leftover wheat in a farmer's field. The farmer is Boaz, who turns out to be Naomi's relative. Although Ruth is an outsider, Boaz is kind to her and lets her work in safety. At that time, the closest relative

The first people to hear or read this story were Jewish. They would have known straight away that Ruth, from Moab, was an outsider, even an enemy. Is the ending surprising?

had a duty to marry a woman whose husband had died. So Ruth reminds Boaz that he should marry her! Boaz says that there is another relative who is even closer. After this man turns Ruth down, Boaz and Ruth get married. Their great-grandson is David, whose story starts in R26.

Q Have you moved to a new town or country? What did you like or dislike about it? Who made you feel welcome?

R25 Who is it?

The *Israelites* are still led by judges and also have *priests*, who live at God's special place in Shiloh. A woman called Hannah goes to Shiloh and prays so hard – she's desperate to have a baby. God hears her prayer, and within a year, Samuel is born. While he's still young, Samuel goes to live in Shiloh.

1 SAMUEL 3:1–10

1–2 Samuel served the LORD by helping Eli the priest, who was by that time almost blind. In those days, the LORD hardly ever spoke directly to people, and he did not appear to them in dreams very often. But one night, Eli was asleep in his room, **3** and Samuel was sleeping on a mat near the **sacred chest** in the LORD's house. They had not been asleep very long **4** when the LORD called out Samuel's name.

"Here I am!" Samuel answered.

5 Then he ran to Eli and said, "Here I am. What do you want?"

"I didn't call you," Eli answered. "Go back to bed."

Samuel went back.

6 Again the LORD called out Samuel's name. Samuel got up and went to Eli. "Here I am," he said. "What do you want?"

Eli told him, "Son, I didn't call you. Go back to sleep."

7 The LORD had not spoken to Samuel before, and Samuel did not recognize the voice. **8** When the LORD called out his name for the third time, Samuel went to Eli again and said, "Here I am. What do you want?"

Eli finally realized that it was the LORD who was speaking to Samuel. **9** So he said, "Go back and lie down! If someone speaks to you again, answer, 'I'm listening, LORD. What do you want me to do?'"

Once again Samuel went back and lay down.

10 The LORD then stood beside Samuel and called out as he had done before, "Samuel! Samuel!"

"I'm listening," Samuel answered. "What do you want me to do?"

> 1 Samuel is one of several books in the Bible that have numbers in front of them! This is because there is more than one book written by, or to, the same person, or about the same period of history. How many numbered Bible books can you find in *Into the Bible*?

Q Why doesn't Samuel recognise God's voice straight away? What do you think God's voice sounds like?

David

⭐ Star factor

★ **Passionate – about God, life and his people**

Key Bible verse
You, Lord, are my shepherd.
I will never be in need.
Psalm 23:1 (R35)

Big events in David's life

Biggest shock	Chosen by God when he was still young (R26)
Bravest	Fought a giant soldier – and won (R27)
Most scary	Had to run from jealous King Saul
Most loyal	Had a chance to kill King Saul but didn't take it
Most powerful	Became king of the whole of Israel
Worst	Had a brave soldier killed so he could marry the soldier's wife (R28)
Saddest	His own son tried to take over the country and forced David out

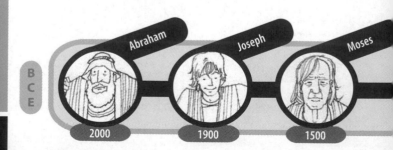

Abraham   Joseph   Moses

B
C
E

2000   1900   1500

What the Bible says about David

★ He loved God

★ He was good-looking (R26)

★ He was a great musician and probably wrote the most famous songs in the Bible (R35)

★ He was a good leader

★ He was fair

★ He acted without thinking (R28)

And in the rest of the world…

Which three would have been true in 1000BCE?

A Iron has been discovered – a metal stronger than bronze.

B Roman alphabet (which you are reading) has been written down.

C Hebrew and Greek alphabets have been written down.

D Stone cities are being built in Mexico.

E Potatoes have been brought to Britain.

Answers upside down, bottom of page

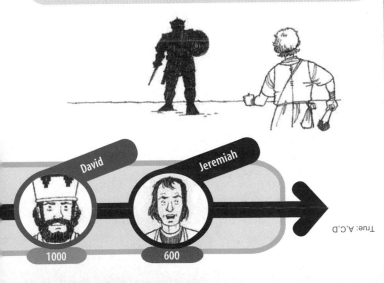

True: A,C,D

David   Jeremiah

1000   600

How to choose a king

Samuel (R25) becomes a leader of the Israelites. When he is older, the Israelites ask for a king. God allows this, and Samuel chooses Saul. Saul starts as a good king but he disobeys God. So God tells Samuel to choose a new king.

1 SAMUEL 16:4–13

4 Samuel did what the LORD told him and went to Bethlehem. The town leaders went to meet him, but they were terribly afraid and asked, "Is this a friendly visit?"

5 "Yes, it is!" Samuel answered. "I've come to offer a **sacrifice** to the LORD. Get yourselves ready to take part in the sacrifice and come with me." Samuel also invited Jesse and his sons to come to the sacrifice, and he got them ready to take part.

6 When Jesse and his sons arrived, Samuel noticed Jesse's eldest son, Eliab. "He must be the one the LORD has chosen," Samuel said to himself.

7 But the LORD told him, "Samuel, don't think Eliab is the one just because he's tall and handsome. He isn't the one I've chosen. People judge others by what they look like, but I judge people by what is in their hearts."

8 Jesse told his son Abinadab to go over to Samuel, but Samuel said, "No, the LORD hasn't chosen him."

9 Next, Jesse sent his son Shammah to him, and Samuel said, "The LORD hasn't chosen him either."

10 Jesse sent all seven of his sons over to Samuel. Finally, Samuel said, "Jesse, the LORD hasn't chosen any of these young men. **11** Do you have any more sons?"

"Yes," Jesse answered. "My youngest son David is out taking care of the sheep."

"Send for him!" Samuel said. "We won't start the ceremony until he gets here."

12 Jesse sent for David. He was a healthy, good-looking boy with a sparkle in his eyes. As soon as David came, the LORD told Samuel, "He's the one! Get up and pour the **olive**

oil on his head."

13 Samuel poured the oil on David's head while his brothers watched. At that moment, the **Spirit of the** LORD took control of David and stayed with him from then on. Samuel returned home to Ramah.

> **Q** What qualities would a good king of Israel need?

> **Q** When someone meets you for the first time, what do they see?

The champion!

King Saul and his army are facing their worst enemy. The Philistine army has two advantages over Israel – iron weapons, and Goliath, a soldier who is three metres tall. David arrives and hears what Goliath is saying about God and the Israelites. David is angry and offers to fight Goliath. Saul gives David his armour, but this isn't what David needs.

1 SAMUEL 17:39–51

David took off the armour 40 and picked up his shepherd's stick. He went out to a stream and picked up five smooth stones and put them in his leather bag. Then with his **sling** in his hand, he went straight towards Goliath.

41 Goliath came towards David, walking behind the soldier who was carrying his shield. 42 When Goliath saw that David was just a healthy, good-looking boy, he made fun of him. 43 "Do you think I'm a dog?" Goliath asked. "Is that why you've come after me with a stick?" He cursed David in the name of the Philistine gods 44 and shouted, "Come on! When I'm finished with you, I'll feed you to the birds and wild animals!"

45 David answered:

You've come out to fight me with a sword and a spear and a dagger. But I've come out to fight you in the name of the LORD All-Powerful. He is the God of Israel's army, and you have insulted him too!

David's work as a shepherd meant sleeping rough in the desert and saving his sheep from bears or lions.

46 Today the LORD will help me defeat you. I'll knock you down and cut off your head, and I'll feed the bodies of the other Philistine soldiers to the birds and wild animals. Then the whole world will know that Israel has a real God.

47 Everybody here will see that the LORD doesn't need swords or spears to save his people. The LORD always wins his battles, and he will help us defeat you.

48 When Goliath started forward, David ran towards him. **49** He put a stone in his sling and swung the sling around by its straps. When he let go of one strap, the stone flew out and hit Goliath on the forehead. It cracked his skull, and he fell face down on the ground. **50** David defeated Goliath with a sling and a stone. He killed him without even using a sword.

51 David ran over and pulled out Goliath's sword. Then he used it to cut off Goliath's head.

When the Philistines saw what had happened to their hero, they started running away.

Q What do you notice about what David says to Goliath?

Q Why was David so confident?

The king's choice

David kills Goliath and becomes a soldier in Saul's army. Saul gets jealous, and tries to kill David. So David has to hide, along with the people who support him. But he won't kill Saul. After Saul dies in battle, David becomes king. He makes Jerusalem his capital city, and brings back *the sacred chest* so that people can worship God. Everything seems to be going well until...

2 SAMUEL 11:1–6, 26–27

1 It was now spring, the time when kings go to war. David sent out the whole Israelite army under the command of Joab and his officers. They destroyed the Ammonite army and surrounded the capital city of Rabbah, but David stayed in **Jerusalem.**

2-4 Late one afternoon, David got up from a nap and was walking around on the flat roof of his palace. A beautiful young woman was down below in her courtyard, bathing as her religion required. David happened to see her, and he sent one of his servants to find out who she was.

The servant came back and told David, "Her name is Bathsheba. She is the daughter of Eliam, and she is the wife of Uriah the Hittite."

David sent some messengers to bring her to his palace. She came to him, and he slept with her. Then she returned home. **5** But later, when she found out that she was going to have a baby, she sent someone to David with this message: "I'm pregnant!"

6 David sent a message to Joab: "Send Uriah the Hittite to me."

The story continues...

David tries to cover up the fact that Bathsheba is pregnant by getting her husband Uriah to go home and sleep with his wife – so Uriah will think that it's his baby. But Uriah refuses to go home – he wants to stay on duty as a soldier. So David sends Uriah to the fiercest part of the fighting, where he is killed.

26 When Bathsheba heard that her husband was dead, she mourned for him. **27** Then after the time for mourning was over, David sent someone to bring her to the palace. She became David's wife, and they had a son.

The LORD was angry at what David had done…

The story continues…

The LORD sends **Nathan** the **prophet** to David – and he tells David a story! David realises the story is about him, and at last he sees that he has let God down. He tells God how sorry he is, and later he writes his feelings down (R36).

R36

R20

Q David knew God's rules about marriage and murder. Why do you think he disobeyed God?

Q When you hear bad things about people that you trust, how does it make you feel?

R29

The people's choice

1 Kings 18:20–39

R19

David dies and his son Solomon becomes king. Solomon builds a great *temple*. He is famous for his wealth and wisdom, but he forgets God. After he dies, the country splits into two parts, Israel and Judah. Some kings follow God's ways and try to lead people to follow God too. Some kings follow the gods of other tribes, and the people do the same. God wants them to remember their agreement and sends *prophets* to Israel and Judah to remind them to obey God. One example is Jeremiah – see page 84). *Elijah* is a prophet in Israel at the time of King Ahab. Ahab does not live his life nor worship God as God wants him to. He sees Elijah as an enemy.

20 Ahab got everyone together, then they went to meet Elijah on Mount Carmel. **21** Elijah stood in front of them and said, "How much longer will you try to have things both ways? If the LORD is God, **worship** him! But if Baal is God, worship him!"

Baal and Asherah were names of gods of neighbouring countries and tribes.

The people did not say a word.
22 Then Elijah continued:

I am the LORD's only prophet, but Baal has four hundred and fifty prophets.

23 Bring us two bulls. Baal's prophets can take one of them, kill it, and cut it into pieces. Then they can put the meat on the wood without lighting the fire. I will do the same thing with the other bull, and I won't light a fire under it either.

24 The prophets of Baal will pray to their god, and I will pray to the LORD. The one who answers by starting the fire is God.

"That's a good idea," everyone agreed.

25 Elijah said to Baal's prophets, "There are more of you, so you go first. Pick out a bull and get it ready, but don't light the fire. Then pray to your god."

26 They chose their bull, then they got it ready and prayed to Baal all morning, asking him to start the fire. They danced around the **altar** and shouted, "Answer us, Baal!" But there was no answer.

27 At midday, Elijah began making fun of them. "Pray louder!" he said.

"Baal must be a god. Perhaps he's daydreaming or using the toilet or travelling somewhere. Or perhaps he's asleep, and you have to wake him up."

28 The prophets kept shouting louder and louder, and they cut themselves with swords and knives until they were bleeding. This was the way they worshipped, **29** and they kept it up all afternoon. But there was no answer of any kind.

30 Elijah told everyone to gather around him while he repaired the LORD 's altar. **31–32** Then he used twelve stones to build an altar in honour of the LORD. Each stone stood for one of the tribes of Israel, which was the name the LORD had given to their ancestor **Jacob**. Elijah dug a ditch around the altar, large enough to hold almost fourteen litres.
33 He placed the wood on the altar, then they cut the bull into pieces and laid the meat on the wood.

He told the people, "Fill four large jars with water and pour it over the meat and the wood." After they did this, **34** he told them to do it two more times. They did exactly as he said **35** until finally, the water ran down the altar and filled the ditch.

36 When it was time for the evening sacrifice, Elijah prayed:

Our LORD, you are the God of Abraham, Isaac, and Israel. Now, prove that you are the God of this nation, and that I, your servant, have done this at your command. **37** Please answer me, so these people will know that you are the LORD God, and that you will turn their hearts back to you.

38 The LORD immediately sent fire, and it burnt up the **sacrifice**, the wood, and the stones. It scorched the ground everywhere around the altar and dried up every drop of water in the ditch. **39** When the crowd saw what had happened, they all bowed down and shouted, "The LORD is God! The LORD is God!"

Q If you were Elijah, what would you say God is like?

God speaks

At Mount Carmel, Elijah sees what God can do. But the king is a powerful enemy, and Elijah feels scared and alone...

1 KINGS 19:1–9,11–16

1 Ahab told his wife Jezebel what Elijah had done and that he had killed the prophets.
2 She sent a message to Elijah: "You killed my prophets. Now I'm going to kill you! I pray that the gods will punish me even more severely if I don't do it by this time tomorrow."

R19, 20

3 Elijah was afraid when he got her message, and he ran to the town of Beersheba in Judah. He left his servant there, **4** then walked another whole day into the desert. Finally, he came to a large bush and sat down in its shade. He begged the LORD, "I've had enough. Just let me die! I'm no better off than my ancestors." **5** Then he lay down in the shade and fell asleep.

Suddenly an angel woke him up and said, "Get up and eat." **6** Elijah looked around, and by his head was a jar of water and some baked bread. He sat up, ate and drank, then lay down and went back to sleep.

7 Soon the LORD 's **angel** woke him again and said, "Get up and eat, or else you'll get too tired to travel." **8** So Elijah sat up and ate and drank.

The food and water made him strong enough to walk forty more days. At last, he reached Mount Sinai, the mountain of God, **9** and he spent the night there in a cave...

11 All at once, a strong wind shook the mountain and shattered the rocks. But the LORD was not in the wind. Next, there was

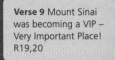

Verse 9 Mount Sinai was becoming a VIP – Very Important Place! R19,20

an earthquake, but the LORD was not in the earthquake.
12 Then there was a fire, but the LORD was not in the fire.

Finally, there was a gentle breeze, **13** and when Elijah heard it, he covered his face with his coat. He went out and stood at the entrance to the cave.

The LORD asked, "Elijah, why are you here?"

14 Elijah answered, "LORD God All-Powerful, I've always done my best to obey you. But your people have broken their solemn promise to you. They have torn down your **altars** and killed all your prophets, except me. And now they are even trying to kill me!"

15 The LORD said:

Elijah, you can go back to the desert near Damascus. And when you get there, appoint Hazael to be king of Syria. **16** Then appoint Jehu son of Nimshi to be king of Israel, and Elisha son of Shaphat to take your place as my prophet.

Q What colours would you choose if you were painting Elijah's meeting with God?

Q Looking at R29 and R30, what do you think were the good and the not-so-good things about being a prophet ?

Discovery

About 300 years have passed since King David led the Israelites. The country has divided into two kingdoms, Israel and Judah. The kings and people of Israel have ignored their agreement with God (R19). God has allowed Israel (the Northern Kingdom) to be invaded by Assyria (from the north). People are taken away as prisoners. Look at the map on page 97. Judah (the Southern Kingdom) is saved from attack, but the people start to forget about God again, until...

1 **Josiah** was eight years old when he became king of Judah, and he ruled thirty-one years from Jerusalem …

2 Josiah always obeyed the LORD, just as his ancestor **David** had done.

3 After Josiah had been king for eighteen years, he told Shaphan, one of his highest officials:

> Go to the LORD 's temple **4** and ask Hilkiah the **high priest** to collect from the guards all the money that the people have donated. **5** Tell Hilkiah to give it to the men supervising the repairs to the **temple**. They can use some of the money to pay **6** the workers, and with the rest of it they can buy wood and stone for the repair work. **7** They are honest, so we won't ask them to keep track of the money.

8 While Shaphan was at the temple, Hilkiah handed him a book and said, "Look what I found here in the temple—*The Book of God's Law*."

Shaphan read it, **9** then went back to Josiah and reported, "Your officials collected the money in the temple and gave it to the men supervising the repairs. **10** But there's something else, Your Majesty. The priest Hilkiah gave me this book." Then Shaphan read it out loud.

11 When Josiah heard what was in *The Book of God's Law*, he tore his clothes in sorrow. **12** At once he called together Hilkiah, Shaphan, Ahikam son of Shaphan, Achbor son of Micaiah, and his own servant Asaiah. He said, **13** "The LORD must be furious with me and everyone else in Judah, because our ancestors did not obey the laws written in this book. Go and find out what the LORD wants us to do."

Josiah brought about many changes in Judah. He destroyed the places where idols were worshipped, he encouraged the people to worship God as God wanted and reminded them of all that God had done for them in the past. But his reforms did not last. After he died, armies invaded from Egypt (from the south) and then Babylon (from the east). Eventually, the Babylonian army burned Jerusalem, and led nearly all the people away as prisoners to Babylon.

But Josiah's faith helped his people. In exile in Babylon, they remembered God. They wrote songs (for example, R37) and wrote down the amazing things that God had done. God didn't forget them either.

Verse 11 Tearing your clothes was a sign of strong emotion – anger or sadness

The story continues...

The prophetess, Huldah, told this to Josiah:

18 "Josiah, listen to what I am going to do. **19** I noticed how sad you were when you read that this country and its people would be completely wiped out. You even tore your clothes in sorrow, and I heard you cry. **20** So I will let you die in peace, before I destroy this place."

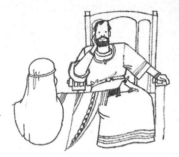

R26, R27

The story continues...

50 years later Josiah is dead. But Jerusalem has been destroyed and God's people have been taken to Babylon. (See NSEW page 73.)

> **Q** Are you older or younger than Josiah when he became king (verse 1)? If you became ruler of your country, what changes would you make? Who would you get as your advisers?

R32 Going home

The people are in *exile* in Babylon, but God hasn't forgotten them. Daniel, who is from one of the leading Jewish families, becomes an important leader in Babylon. He discovers that God is with him, even in a lions' den. Then, after seventy years, King Cyrus of Babylon allows some Jews to return to Jerusalem. They rebuild the *temple*, but *Jerusalem* is still a dangerous place. Many more years pass. Back in Babylon, an important Jew called Nehemiah hears about Jerusalem's troubles and starts praying...

1 During the month of Nisan in the twentieth year that Artaxerxes was king, I served him his wine, as I had done before. But this was the first time I had ever looked depressed. **2** So the king said, "Why do you look so sad? You're not sick. Something must be bothering you."

Even though I was frightened, **3** I answered, "Your Majesty, I hope you live for ever! I feel sad because the city where my ancestors are buried is in ruins, and its gates have been burnt down."

4 The king asked, "What do you want me to do?"

I prayed to the God who rules from **heaven**. **5** Then I told the king, "Sir, if it's all right with you, please send me back to Judah, so that I can rebuild the city where my ancestors are buried."

6 The queen was sitting beside the king when he asked me, "How long will it take, and when will you be back?" The king agreed to let me go, and I told him when I would return…

11 Three days after arriving in Jerusalem, **12** I got up during the night and left my house. I took some men with me, without telling anyone what I thought God wanted me to do for the city. The only animal I took was the donkey I rode on. **13** I went through Valley Gate on the west, then south past Dragon Spring, before coming to Rubbish Gate. As I rode along, I took a good look at the crumbled walls of the city and the gates that had been torn down and burnt. **14** On the east side of the city, I headed north to Fountain Gate and King's Pool, but then the path became too narrow for my donkey. **15** So I went down to Kidron Valley

> **Verse 2** The king's servants were meant to look happy, all the time! Nehemiah could have lost his job (or worse) by looking sad.

and looked at the wall from there. Then before daylight I returned to the city through Valley Gate.

16 None of the city officials knew what I had in mind. And I had not even told any of the Jews—not the priests, the leaders, the officials, or any other Jews who would be helping in the work. **17** But when I got back, I said to them, "Jerusalem is truly in a mess! The gates have been torn down and burnt, and everything is in ruins. We must rebuild the city wall so that we can again take pride in our city."

18 Then I told them how kind God had been and what the king had said.

Immediately, they replied, "Let's start building now!" So they got everything ready.

Over 400 years follow before the first events of the **New Testament**. During this time the **Greek** army attacked the Jewish people, ruled their country and treated them harshly. The Romans followed the Greeks and they were ruling the land when Jesus was born.

The story continues...

Nehemiah organises the whole city to rebuild the wall, and writes a long list of everyone who helps. Even when their enemies threaten, they carry on and finish the wall. The Jews celebrate, and sign an agreement to obey the LORD.
They've come back to the country that God promised. They have learnt about obeying God. But they are still waiting for a special person – the **Messiah** – to bring about the real freedom that God plans.
The Old Testament library now starts moving on to poetry...

R39,
R41

Q Nehemiah had never lived in Jerusalem. Why did he want to go back to help?

Q Who makes your area a safer place to live?

Psalms

Psing a Psong!

Psalms (sounds like 'Sarms')

★ is a book of 150 songs to God (the words, not the tunes).

★ are for telling God when you're happy or sad, saying sorry or shouting 'thank you!'

★ are still sung by Jewish and Christian believers.

★ can be a few lines, or several pages.

Many of the Psalms are linked to the life of King David (see David: IP4, page 62) and it's likely that he wrote some of them.

> In the psalms that follow, you can find someone who…
>
> a) is amazed by the world
> b) thinks God is like a shepherd
> c) thinks God's words last forever
> d) is sorry
> e) is a prisoner in their enemy's country
> f) trusts God to keep them safe
> g) writes about the sun
>
> *Answers upside down, bottom of page*

a = 8, b = 23, c = 19, d = 51, e = 137, f = 23, g = 19

A beautiful world

This psalm uses lots of images that come from creation.

PSALM 8

1 Our LORD and Ruler,
your name is wonderful everywhere on earth!
You let your **glory** be seen in the heavens above.

2 With praises from children and from tiny infants,
you have built a fortress.
It makes your enemies silent,
and all who turn against you are left speechless.

3 I often think of the heavens your hands have made,
and of the moon and stars you put in place.

4 Then I ask, "Why do you care about us humans?
Why are you concerned for us weaklings?"
5 You made us a little lower than you yourself,
and you have crowned us with glory and honour.

6 You let us rule everything your hands have made.
And you put all of it under our power—
7 the sheep and the cattle, and every wild animal,
8 the birds in the sky, the fish in the sea, and all ocean
creatures.

9 Our LORD and Ruler, your name is wonderful everywhere
on earth!

Q Is there a place near your home where you can see for a
long way? Next time you're there, think about what you see
(even if it's a big city). Maybe make up a song about it!

Songs are for singing

Worshippers used this psalm, probably written by King David, to celebrate the wonders of the world God has made and the guidance he has given for living.

PSALM 19:1–8

1 The heavens keep telling the wonders of God,
and the skies declare what he has done.
2 Each day informs the following day; each night announces to the next.
3 They don't speak a word and there is never the sound of a voice.
4 Yet their message reaches all the earth,
and it travels around the world.

In the heavens a tent is set up for the sun.
5 It rises like a bridegroom and gets ready like a hero eager to run a race.
6 It travels all the way across the sky.
Nothing hides from its heat.

7 The **Law** of the LORD is perfect; it gives us new life.
His teachings last for ever, and they give wisdom
to ordinary people.
8 The LORD's instruction is right; it makes our hearts glad.
His commands shine brightly, and they give us light.

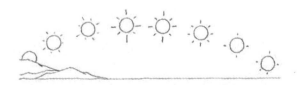

Q God speaks to people through the world he created and through his law, the Bible. Can you put this psalm into your own words?

God as a shepherd

God is often pictured as something people can see in their world, such as a strong tower or an eagle. Here King David, who wrote this psalm, pictures God as a shepherd.

R26,R27

Lost sheep
R 76
Good
shepherd
R83

PSALM 23

1 You, LORD, are my shepherd.
I will never be in need.
2 You let me rest in fields of
green grass. You lead me to streams
of peaceful water, **3** and you
refresh my life.

You are true to your name,
and you lead me
along the right paths.
4 I may walk through valleys
as dark as death,
but I won't be afraid.
You are with me, and your
shepherd's rod
makes me feel safe.

5 You treat me to a feast,
while my enemies watch.
You honour me as your guest,
and you fill my cup until it overflows.

6 Your kindness and love will always be with me
each day of my life, and I will live for ever in your house,
LORD.

Q What pictures does this psalm/song paint in your mind?

Sorry

King David, who'd promised to obey God, has messed up
(R28). He's broken God's rules about marriage and murder,
and he can never put things right again. He realises the
distance between him and God, because of the bad stuff he's
done. The Bible says that these are David's words...

PSALM 51

1 You are kind, God! Please have pity on me. You are always
merciful! Please wipe away my **sins**.
2 Wash me clean from all of my sin and guilt.
3 I know about my sins, and I cannot forget my terrible guilt.
4 You are really the one I have sinned against; I have
disobeyed you and have done wrong. So it is right and fair
for you to correct and punish me.

5 I have sinned and done wrong since the day I was born.
6 But you want complete honesty, so teach me true wisdom.
7 Wash me with hyssop until I am clean and whiter than
snow.
8 Let me be happy and joyful! You crushed my bones, now
let them celebrate.
9 Turn your eyes from my sin and cover my guilt.
10 Create pure thoughts in me and make me faithful again.
11 Don't chase me away from you or take your **Holy Spirit**
away from me.

12 Make me as happy as you did when you saved me; make
me want to obey!
13 I will teach sinners your **Law**, and they will return to you.
14 Keep me from any deadly sin. Only you can save me!
Then I will shout and sing about your power to save.

15 Help me to speak, and I will praise you, LORD.
16 **Offerings** and **sacrifices** are not what you want.
17 The way to please you is to feel sorrow deep in our
hearts. This is the kind of sacrifice you won't refuse.

18 Please be willing, LORD, to help the city of **Zion** and to rebuild its walls.

19 Then you will be pleased with the proper sacrifices, and we will offer bulls on your **altar** once again.

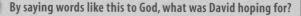

Q By saying words like this to God, what was David hoping for?

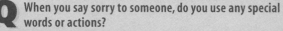

Q When you say sorry to someone, do you use any special words or actions?

Songs full of sadness

The people of God sang this sad psalm when they had been forced to leave *Jerusalem* and go to *Babylon*.

FROM PSALM 137

1 Beside the rivers of **Babylon** we thought about **Jerusalem**, and we sat down and cried.

2 We hung our small harps on the willow trees.

3 Our enemies had brought us here as their prisoners, and now they wanted us to sing and entertain them They insulted us and shouted, "Sing about **Zion**!"

4 Here in a foreign land, how can we sing about the LORD?

Q How do songs help you express what you are feeling?

Whatever?

It's around 1000, maybe 900 BCE. A writer – a rich and clever man – is fed up and can't make sense of life. If he was being interviewed, he'd probably say, 'Whatever!' He starts writing his thoughts for others to read. Suddenly he breaks out into this poem...

ECCLESIASTES 3:1–11

1 Everything on earth has its own time and its own season.
2 There is a time for birth and death, planting and reaping,
3 for killing and healing, destroying and building,
4 for crying and laughing, weeping and dancing,
5 for throwing stones and gathering stones, embracing and parting.
6 There is a time for finding and losing, keeping and giving,
7 for tearing and sewing, listening and speaking.
8 There is also a time for love and hate, for war and peace.
9 What do we gain by all our hard work? **10** I have seen what difficult things God demands of us. **11** God makes everything happen at the right time. Yet none of us can ever fully understand all he has done, and he puts questions in our minds about the past and the future.

Wisdom In Middle Eastern lands (see map page 97), wisdom was really valued at this time. It helped people know how to live. Israel's King Solomon was known throughout the world for his wisdom. Some of these wise thoughts are recorded in the Old Testament, in the books of Job, Proverbs and Ecclesiastes.

The story continues...

After writing this amazing poem, the writer goes back to being fed up!

Q What would you put in a poem about the times or events in your life?

Jeremiah

⭐ Star factor

★ Stuck at it, even when it was tough

Key Bible verse

Jeremiah, I am your Creator, and before you were born, I chose you to speak for me…
Jeremiah 1:5 (R42)

Big events in Jeremiah's life

Muddiest	His enemies threw him into a well
Friendliest	Ebedmelech from Ethiopia rescued him from the well
Most honest	Told God that he was totally fed up with his job
Scariest	Arrested by royal officers and threatened with the death penalty
Saddest	Saw his own words come true, when Jerusalem was invaded (R31)
Most hopeful	Looked ahead to the time when God would start a new agreement (R45)

And in the rest of the world…

The first Olympics took place in 776 BCE.

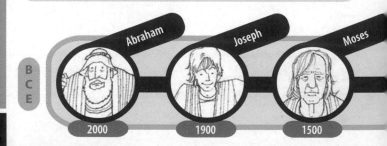

B C E

Abraham — 2000
Joseph — 1900
Moses — 1500

What the Bible says about Jeremiah

★ He became a prophet when he was young (R42)

★ He didn't get married or have children

★ He was a priest as well as a prophet

★ He told the people they would be in exile in Babylon for 70 years

★ He went into exile with the people, though he could have stayed

Prophets in *Into the Bible*

Elijah
(R29–R30)
Isaiah
(R39–R42)
Jeremiah
(R43–R45)
Amos (R46)
Jonah (R47)
John the
Baptist (R50)

About one third of Old Testament books are prophecy, and many of these verses are quoted in the New Testament by Jesus and his followers.

WANTED
A PROPHET

★ To listen to God
★ To tell people what God expects now
★ (Sometimes) to look ahead to what God will do in the future

WARNING
You may be killed, locked up, ignored or lonely

REWARD
Some people may listen and change. (2500 years later, people will still hear God's message through your words...)

David — 1000

Jeremiah — 600

Animal kingdom

R26, 27
David–IP4,
page 62

Isaiah the *prophet* (740–680BCE) sees God! He is so amazed by this that he spends his life passing God's messages on to the people who lived in *Judah*. This is at a time when *Israel*, in the north, is being invaded by Assyria. Some of Isaiah's messages are about how God's people should be living. Others are about God and his plans for the future...

Many of Isaiah's messages appear again – in the **New Testament**. The first believers in Jesus looked back at the Old Testament to see how the words of Isaiah and other prophets came true in the things that Jesus did and said.

ISAIAH 11:1–6

1 Like a branch that sprouts from a stump,
someone from **David**'s family will some day be king.
2 The **Spirit of the** LORD will be with him
to give him understanding, wisdom, and insight.
He will be powerful, and he will know and honour the LORD.
3 His greatest joy will be to obey the LORD.

This king won't judge by appearances or listen to rumours.
4 The poor and the needy
will be treated with fairness and with justice.
His word will be law everywhere in the land,
and criminals will be put to death.
5 Honesty and fairness will be his royal robes.
6 Leopards will lie down with young goats, and wolves will rest with lambs.
Calves and lions will eat together and be cared for by little children.

Q What would it be like to live in this new 'kingdom'?

 Q What would your perfect world look like?

Big questions

People who have ignored Isaiah's messages are now in captivity, and asking questions. What is God like? Has he forgotten us? The prophet gives them answers – by asking more questions...

ISAIAH 40:12–14, 25–31

12 Did any of you measure the ocean by yourself or stretch out the sky with your own hands?
Did you put the soil of the earth in a bucket or weigh the hills and mountains on balance scales?
13 Has anyone told the LORD what he must do or given him advice?
14 Did the LORD ask anyone to teach him wisdom and justice? ...

What is God like? As well as asking the questions, Isaiah gives an answer – he writes about one special person who will show what God is like.

→ R41

25 The holy God asks, "Who compares with me? Is anyone my equal?"
26 Look at the evening sky! Who created the stars? Who gave them each a name? Who leads them like an army? The LORD is so powerful that none of the stars are ever missing.
27 You people of Israel, say, "God pays no attention to us! He doesn't care if we are treated unjustly." But how can you say that?
28 Don't you know? Haven't you heard?
The LORD is the **eternal** God, Creator of the earth.
He never gets weary or tired; his wisdom cannot be measured.
29 The LORD gives strength to those who are weary.
30 Even young people get tired, then stumble and fall.
31 But those who trust the LORD will find new strength.
They will be strong like eagles soaring upward on wings; they will walk and run without getting tired.

 How would you answer the question, "What is God like?"

God's servant 1

The Israelites know about being servants or slaves. They are prisoners in Babylon, and have to work for foreign owners. The prophet describes how the Israelites are to be 'servants' of God. And he describes God's special servant, someone in the future who will show what God is like.

ISAIAH 53:7–10

7 He was painfully abused, but he did not complain.
He was silent like a lamb being led to the butcher,
as quiet as a sheep having its wool cut off.

8 He was condemned to death without a fair trial. Who could have imagined what would happen to him? His life was taken away because of the sinful things my people had done.

9 He wasn't dishonest or violent, but he was buried in a tomb of cruel and rich people.

10 The LORD decided his servant would suffer as a **sacrifice** to take away the **sin** and guilt of others. Now the servant will live to see his own **descendants**. He did everything the LORD had planned.

R59

R2, R21

R44

Although God created people to be like him, they went their own way. This is called sin. Moses gave God's directions for people to be forgiven by offering animals as sacrifices. Isaiah now says that a person will become the sacrifice, taking the punishment that the rest of the people deserved.

Q Why would someone be willing to serve God, even if it meant dying?

God's servant 2

The story continues, as Isaiah speaks of what will happen when the Messiah, the promised one from God, will come. This is what he will say.

ISAIAH 61:1–2

1 The Spirit of the LORD God has taken control of me! The LORD has chosen and sent me to tell the oppressed the good news,

to heal the brokenhearted, and to announce freedom for prisoners and captives.

2 This is the year when the LORD will show kindness to us and punish our enemies.

> **Verses 1 and 2** Jesus spoke of himself in this way in Luke 4:18,19 (not in *Into the Bible*). See page 17 (introduction)

Too young?

Think about a famous speaker – a politician, a celebrity, your teacher… Have you ever wondered how they started out? What was the series of events that changed them to the person that's so well known? Maybe they started out as young as Jeremiah! (620–580BCE)

(See Jeremiah:IP5, page 84)

JEREMIAH 1:4–10

4 The LORD said,

5 "Jeremiah, I am your Creator, and before you were born, I chose you to speak for me to the nations."

6 I replied, "I'm not a good speaker, LORD, and I'm too young."

← R31, R32

7 The LORD answered, "Don't say you're too young. If I tell you to go and speak to someone, then go! And when I tell you what to say, don't leave out a word! **8** I promise to be with you and keep you safe, so don't be afraid." **9** The LORD reached out his hand, then he touched my mouth and said, "I am giving you the words to say, **10** and I am sending you with authority to speak to the nations for me. You will tell them of doom and destruction and of rising and rebuilding again."

> Jeremiah starts speaking during a great time for Judah, when Josiah was king. He continues through the saddest and most difficult time of his country's history, just before God's people were dragged off into exile in Babylon.

Q Have you ever been asked to do something that you'd never done before? Did you accept or turn it down? What helped you make your decision?

R44

A message from the potter

Jeremiah keeps listening to God, and passing on the messages that he hears – even if it makes him unpopular. Many of his messages are linked to everyday places or objects. At a time when every plate, cup and bowl was made from clay, he gives this message at one of the busiest and best-known places in town.

JEREMIAH 18:1–13,18

1 The LORD told me, **2** "Go to the pottery shop, and when you get there, I will tell you what to say to the people."

3 I went there and saw the potter making clay pots on his pottery wheel. **4** And whenever the clay would not take the shape he wanted, he would change his mind and form it into some other shape.

5 Then the LORD told me to say:

6 People of Israel, I, the LORD, have power over you, just as a potter has power over clay. **7** If I threaten to uproot and shatter an evil nation **8** and that nation turns from its evil, I will change my mind.

9 If I promise to make a nation strong, **10** but its people start disobeying me and doing evil, then I will change my mind and not help them at all.

11 So listen to me, people of **Judah** and **Jerusalem**! I have decided to strike you with disaster, and I won't change my mind unless you stop sinning and start living right.

12 But I know you won't listen. You might as well answer, "We don't care what you say. We have made plans to sin, and we are going to be stubborn and do what we want!"

13 So I, the LORD, command you to ask the nations, and find out if they have ever heard of such a horrible sin as what you have done.

18 Some of the people said, "Let's get rid of Jeremiah! We will always have **priests** to teach us God's laws, as well as wise people to give us advice, and **prophets** to speak the LORD's messages. So, instead of listening to Jeremiah any longer, let's accuse him of a crime."

Q If Jeremiah was speaking this message in your country today, where might he have gone?

A new agreement

Many years before, God and his people had made an agreement. Jeremiah has to speak out because the people aren't keeping this agreement. The worst thing possible happens. The people don't listen to Jeremiah. They ignore God. Babylon, the most powerful nation in the world at that time, invades their country and takes the people away as slaves. What could Jeremiah say now? I told you so? It serves you right? Or this... ?

R19, R20

JEREMIAH 31:31–34

31 The LORD said: The time will surely come when I will make a new agreement with the people of Israel and Judah.
32 It will be different from the agreement I made with their ancestors when I led them out of Egypt. Although I was their God, they broke that agreement.
33 Here is the new agreement that I, the LORD, will make with the people of Israel: "I will write my laws on their hearts and minds. I will be their God, and they will be my people.
34 "No longer will they have to teach one another to obey me. I, the LORD, promise that all of them will obey me, ordinary people and rulers alike. I will forgive their **sins** and forget the evil things they have done."

Q How is this agreement different from the first agreement that the people found so hard to keep?

Be fair!

Many prophets already work 'full-time' for God as *priests*. Amos, who lived around 760–750BCE, works full-time as a farmer. He leaves his home to speak to people he's never mixed with before – the rich people of Israel. He speaks about the part of God's law that they are ignoring – laws to protect poor people, like Amos!

AMOS 1:1–2

1 I am Amos. And I raised sheep near the town of Tekoa when Uzziah was king of **Judah** and Jeroboam son of Jehoash was king of **Israel.**

Two years before the earthquake, the LORD gave me several messages about Israel, **2** and I said: When the LORD roars from Jerusalem, pasture lands and Mount Carmel dry up and turn brown.

AMOS 2:6–7

6 The LORD said: I will punish Israel for countless crimes, and I won't change my mind. They sell honest people for money, and the needy are sold for the price of sandals. **7** They throw the poor to the ground and push aside those who are helpless.

AMOS 5:6–15

6 Turn back to the LORD, you **descendants** of **Joseph**, and you will live. If you don't, the LORD will attack like fire. Bethel will burn to the ground, and no one can save it. **7** You people are doomed! You twist the truth and trample on justice.

8 But the LORD created the stars and put them in place. He turns darkness to dawn and daylight to darkness; he scoops up the ocean and empties it on the earth. **9** God destroys mighty soldiers and strong fortresses.

10 You people hate judges and honest witnesses; **11** you abuse the poor and demand heavy taxes from them.

You have built expensive homes, but you won't enjoy them; you have planted vineyards, but you will get no wine.

12 I am the LORD, and I know your terrible **sins**.
You cheat honest people and take bribes;
you rob the poor of justice.

13 Times are so evil that anyone with good sense will keep quiet.

14 If you really want to live, you must stop doing wrong and start doing right.
I, the LORD God All-Powerful, will then be on your side, just as you claim I am.

15 Choose good instead of evil! See that justice is done.
Perhaps I, the LORD All-Powerful, will be kind to what's left of your people.

> **Q** How different would life be for poor people if rich people listened to Amos' message?

R47 **Going overboard**

Jonah, who lived around 800–750 BCE, is one of the best-known prophets in the Old Testament. However, unlike other prophets, his message wasn't to the people of Israel, but to their enemies in Nineveh.

JONAH 1:1–17

1 One day the LORD told Jonah, the son of Amittai, **2** to go to the great city of Nineveh and say to the people, "The LORD has seen your terrible **sins**. You are doomed!"

3 Instead, Jonah ran from the LORD. He went to the seaport of Joppa and bought a ticket on a ship that was going to Spain. Then he got on the ship and sailed away to escape.

4 But the LORD made a strong wind blow, and such a bad

storm came up that the ship was about to be broken to pieces. **5** The sailors were frightened, and they all started praying to their gods. They even threw the ship's cargo overboard to make the ship lighter.

All this time, Jonah was down below deck, sound asleep. **6** The ship's captain went to him and said, "How can you sleep at a time like this? Get up and pray to your God! Perhaps he will have pity on us and keep us from drowning."

7 Finally, the sailors got together and said, "Let's ask our gods to show us who caused all this trouble." It turned out to be Jonah.

8 They started asking him, "Are you the one who brought all this trouble on us? What business are you in? Where do you come from? What is your country? Who are your people?"

9 Jonah answered, "I'm a **Hebrew,** and I **worship** the LORD God of **heaven,** who made the sea and the dry land."

10 When the sailors heard this, they were frightened, because Jonah had already told them he was running from the LORD. Then they said, "Do you know what you have done?"

11 The storm kept getting worse, until finally the sailors asked him, "What should we do with you to make the sea calm down?"

12 Jonah told them, "Throw me into the sea, and it will calm down. I'm the cause of this terrible storm."

13 The sailors tried their best to row to the shore. But they could not do it, and the storm kept getting worse every minute. **14** So they prayed to the LORD, "Please don't let us drown for taking this man's life. Don't hold us guilty for killing an innocent man. All this happened because you wanted it to." **15** Then they threw Jonah overboard, and the sea calmed down. **16** The sailors were so terrified that they offered a **sacrifice** to the LORD and made all kinds of promises.

17 The LORD sent a big fish to swallow Jonah, and Jonah was inside the fish for three days and three nights.

The story goes on...

This is a turning point for Jonah. He prays, he is set down, alive, on the shore, and he obeys God. He preaches God's message to Nineveh, and the people there believe him. They start believing in God and God lets them live.

Q What surprises you most about this story?

Jonah isn't the last prophet in the Old Testament. The messages of more prophets are recorded. The Old Testament ends with these words from Malachi (whose name means 'messenger'):

Don't ever forget the laws and teachings I gave my servant **Moses** on Mount Sinai. I, the Lord, promise to send the prophet **Elijah** before that great and terrible day comes. He will lead children and parents to love each other more, so that when I come, I won't bring doom to the land.

Over 400 years follow before the first events of the New Testament. During this time the Old Testament was translated from Hebrew into Greek. Latin, Greek and Hebrew/Aramaic languages were spoken by the time of Jesus. The New Testament, however, was written in Greek.

← R19
R29,R30

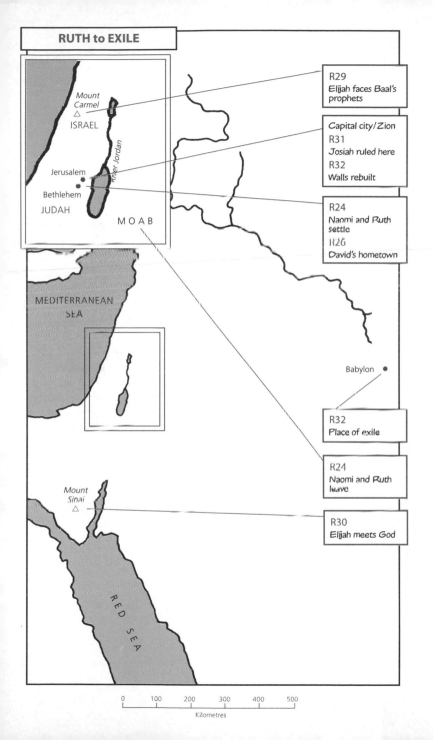

RUTH to EXILE

Mount Carmel △

ISRAEL

River Jordan

Jerusalem ●

Bethlehem ●

JUDAH

MOAB

MEDITERRANEAN SEA

Babylon ●

Mount Sinai △

RED SEA

R29
Elijah faces Baal's prophets

Capital city/Zion
R31
Josiah ruled here
R32
Walls rebuilt

R24
Naomi and Ruth settle
R26
David's hometown

R32
Place of exile

R24
Naomi and Ruth leave

R30
Elijah meets God

0   100   200   300   400   500
Kilometres

The New Testament

Into the Bible contains 10 of the 27 books in the New Testament, the ones written after the birth of Jesus. They are about his life and death and how that affected the rest of the world. These books contain stories, teaching and letters, all written in less than a hundred years after Jesus was born. You will travel through present-day Israel, Syria, Turkey, Greece, Cyprus, Malta and Italy. Like Jonah, Paul also wanted to head off to Spain, and never got there.

The New Testament starts with four gospel accounts. They contain the same story told four times! Just imagine a famous footballer visits your school to take a PE lesson. Afterwards, if you and your friends write about the visit, your accounts will all be different because some of you may have actually spoken to the footballer, some of you may not like football at all and some of you may only be writing down what someone else told you. The four accounts of the life of Jesus are a bit like this. They all tell the same story but told by people who had different experiences of Jesus. They are known as gospels and are named after the people who probably wrote them.

The rest of the New Testament is mainly letters written to Christians in a variety of places and situations. The final book, Revelation (R100–101) is written in colourful language about the conflict between good and evil in the world, now, in the past and in the future.

Matthew, also known as Levi, was Jewish. He became a tax collector for the Romans so was hated by his Jewish neighbours. Then Jesus called Matthew to follow him. Instead of cheating his neighbours, he wrote his account to show them what he had found out. (R48–62)

Mark's gospel is the shortest. Mark was a young man who knew Jesus and later travelled with Paul. Some experts think it was the first to be written, to help Christians in Rome who were being arrested. It's full of the things that Jesus did. Mark wanted his readers to make up their minds about Jesus. People in his book often ask, "Who is this man?" (R63–66)

Luke may have been a Greek doctor who heard about Jesus from Paul (see page 166) Two of his books are in the New Testament. The first is his gospel or account of Jesus' life. His second book is the Acts of the Apostles (R88–94) which is all about what happened to Christians after Jesus went back to heaven. Luke probably wrote for people who weren't Jewish. He recorded Jesus' stories about 'lost' things being found. (R67–79)

John's gospel may have been written by the John who was a fisherman, one of Jesus' closest friends. He told the story of Jesus' life and death, but unlike the other three, he used lots of picture language to help his readers understand who Jesus was. (R80–87)
Towards the end of his book he explained why he was writing:

30 Jesus performed many other miracles for his disciples, and not all of them are written in this book. **31** But these are written so that you will put your faith in Jesus as the Messiah and the Son of God. If you have faith in him, you will have true life. *John 20:30–31*

Mary

⭐ Star factor

★ Trusted God and did
what he asked of her

Key Bible verse

"I am the LORD's servant! Let
it happen as you have said."
Luke 1:38 (R67)

Big events in Mary's life

Bumpiest	Travelled over 100km just before having her first baby (R69)
Scariest	Lost Jesus in Jerusalem when he was 12 (R71)
Hardest	Watched her son die (R86)
Most exciting	Experienced Pentecost 50 days after her son came back to life!
Most amazing	The angel Gabriel appeared to tell her she would give birth to Jesus (R67)
Proudest	Jesus changed water into wine at a wedding

C
E

Mary

Jesus

1st Century

1st Century

What the Bible says about Mary

★ She was a young girl when she became the mother of God's son (R67)

★ She knew about God's promises in the past (R68)

★ Sometimes she told Jesus what to do!

★ She couldn't stop Jesus being killed, but she stayed and watched to the end (R86)

★ Jesus asked his friend John to look after Mary (R86)

More about Mary in the Bible

How Jesus' life and death would affect Mary:
Luke 2:34, 35

At a wedding:
John 2:1–5

About her family:
Mark 6:3

Newsround, 20 BCE

MESSIAH!

The Jews are waiting for their Messiah – a special leader chosen by God. Ruled by Babylonians, Greeks and now Romans, they can't wait for someone to set them free!

I'LL BE BACK!

Britain is still a Roman-free zone, 30 years after Emperor Julius Caesar's attempted takeover. But in the words of the famous governor, 'I'll be back'.

ON PAPER

The Chinese have invented paper – and built the longest wall in the world. But it will be a while before everyone else can read about it!

Peter
1st Century

Paul
1st Century

It's a boy!

Matthew starts his gospel by writing about Jesus' ancestors. He wants Jewish people to think back through their history – through the story told in *Into the Bible* so far – about God's promises to *Abraham*, and *David*, about the *exile* and the return to *Jerusalem*. Now God is doing something new:

MATTHEW 1:18–25

18 This is how Jesus Christ was born.

A young woman named Mary was engaged to **Joseph** from King **David**'s family. But before they were married, she learnt that she was going to have a baby by God's **Holy Spirit**. **19** Joseph was a good man

> **Verse 18** King David – Israel's most famous king up to this point. Joseph lives about 1000 years after David.
> **Verse 22** This prophet was Isaiah.

and did not want to embarrass Mary in front of everyone. So he decided to call off the wedding quietly.

20 While Joseph was thinking about this, an **angel** from the Lord came to him in a dream. The angel said, "Joseph, the baby that Mary will have is from the Holy Spirit. Go ahead and marry her. **21** Then after her baby is born, name him Jesus, because he will save his people from their sins."

22 So the Lord's promise came true, just as the **prophet** had said, **23** "A virgin will have a baby boy, and he will be called Immanuel," which means "God is with us."

24 After Joseph woke up, he and Mary were soon married, just as the Lord's angel had told

Names for Jesus
Jesus – the Greek form of Joshua, a common Jewish boy's name, meaning 'the Lord saves'.
Christ – wasn't Jesus' surname! It's the Greek word for **Messiah**, meaning 'the anointed one' (R26), the title given to Jesus.
Immanuel – this name wasn't given to the baby. But Matthew mentions it, as it tells the reader something important about Jesus.

him to do. **25** But they did not sleep together before her baby was born. Then Joseph named him Jesus.

> **Q** Mary knew that the baby was 'from the Holy Spirit'. Why did Joseph need to hear the same message from an angel?

> **Q** What do you dream about?

Star travellers

R49

Matthew 2:1–12

It's the time of Augustus Caesar and the Romans are in charge of the lands around the Mediterranean – including the small Jewish state of Judea (page 121). Judea has a king called Herod who works for the Romans and is *not* popular.

Elsewhere, early astronomers have decided, as they study the stars, that one star in particular is telling them something that's out of this world.

MATTHEW 2:1–12

1 When Jesus was born in the village of Bethlehem in Judea, Herod was king. During this time some wise men from the east came to Jerusalem **2** and said, "Where is the child born to be king of the Jews? We saw his star in the east and have come to **worship** him."

3 When King Herod heard about this, he was worried, and so was everyone else in **Jerusalem**. **4** Herod brought together the chief **priests** and the teachers of the Law of

> **Verse 1 Bethlehem** – home of King David. Joseph and Mary had to travel to this village because Joseph is from David's tribe and was born in Bethlehem.
> **The east:** the area now covered by Iraq and Iran.

R26

R 69

Moses and asked them, "Where will the **Messiah** be born?"

5 They told him, "He will be born in Bethlehem, just as the **prophet** wrote,

6 'Bethlehem in the land of Judea, you are very important among the towns of Judea. From your town will come a leader, who will be like a shepherd for my people Israel.'"

7 Herod secretly called in the wise men and asked them when they had first seen the star. **8** He told them, "Go to Bethlehem and search carefully for the child. As soon as you find him, let me know. I want to go and worship him too."

9 The wise men listened to what the king said and then left. And the star they had seen in the east went on ahead of them until it stopped over the place where the child was. **10** They were thrilled and excited to see the star.

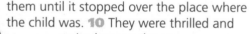

The traveller's gifts
Matthew is writing in a kind of code that his Jewish readers would understand. The expensive gifts all had meanings – gold for a king, frankincense for a priest and myrrh for sadness or death.

11 When the men went into the house and saw the child with Mary, his mother, they knelt down and worshipped him. They took out their gifts of gold, frankincense, and myrrh and gave them to him. **12** Later they were warned in a dream not to return to Herod, and they went back home by another road.

Q Does Matthew tell his readers how many travellers visited Jesus?

Q If you'd been one of the travellers, what presents would you have brought with you?

The journey starts

Herod is jealous of the 'new king' and he orders young boys in Bethlehem to be killed. Joseph escapes to Egypt with Mary and Jesus. When Herod dies, they move to Nazareth in Galilee. Jesus grows up in Nazareth. He learns the same trade as Joseph until he is 30 years old, and ready to start his journey.

Jesus' cousin John has been preparing people for a new message from God. John *baptises* them in the River Jordan as a sign that they want to stop going their own way and start obeying God.

Page 121 for map

MATTHEW 3:13–17

13 Jesus left Galilee and went to the River Jordan to be **baptized** by John. **14** But John kept objecting and said, "I ought to be baptized by you. Why have you come to me?"

15 Jesus answered, "For now this is how it should be, because we must do all that God wants us to do." Then John agreed.

16 So Jesus was baptized. And as soon as he came out of the water, the sky opened, and he saw the **Spirit of God** coming down on him like a dove. **17** Then a voice from heaven said, "This is my own dear Son, and I am pleased with him."

R 62

The Spirit of God, or Holy Spirit, is God: God in a form that can come to a person and change them. The dove is a sign that shows an invisible truth, that Jesus has God's spirit in him. In other words, where Jesus is, God is there too.

Q What does Matthew want to show about Jesus?

How to be happy... ➡

Jesus goes to the town of Capernaum on Lake Galilee. People start to follow him, and he heals people who are unwell. He wants to tell them about the kingdom of heaven – how God wants them to live. He starts with the question, 'Which people are really happy?'

➡

R 72
R65
R66
R53

MATTHEW 5:1–12

1 When Jesus saw the crowds, he went up on the side of a mountain and sat down.

Jesus' **disciples** gathered around him, **2** and he taught them:

3 God blesses those people who depend only on him. They belong to the **kingdom of heaven**!

Verse 1 The hills around Lake Galilee act as a natural 'megaphone'. Someone speaking on the hill, or from a boat on the sea can be heard a long way off.

4 God blesses those people who grieve. They will find comfort!

5 God blesses those people who are humble. The earth will belong to them!

6 God blesses those people who want to obey him more than to eat or drink. They will be given what they want!

Jesus talked on a mountain, where there was lots of space for people to sit. Some Bibles call this 'the Sermon on the Mount' – can you guess why? They call these verses the Beatitudes, which was a word for blessing or happiness in **Latin** Bibles.

7 God blesses those people who are merciful. They will be treated with mercy!

8 God blesses those people whose hearts are pure. They will see him!

9 God blesses those people who make peace. They will be called his children!

10 God blesses those people who are treated badly for doing right. They belong to the kingdom of heaven.

11 God will bless you when people insult you, ill-treat you, and tell all kinds of evil lies about you because of me. **12** Be happy and excited! You will have a great reward in heaven. People did these same things to the **prophets** who lived long ago.

> **Q** How would you answer the question, 'Which people are really happy?'

How to pray

On the mountain, Jesus explains how to do what God wants. This includes talking to God...

MATTHEW 6:9–13
9 You should pray like this:
Our **Father** in **heaven**, help us to honour your name.
10 Come and set up your kingdom, so that everyone on earth will obey you, as you are obeyed in heaven.
11 Give us our food for today.
12 Forgive us for doing wrong, as we forgive others.
13 Keep us from being tempted and protect us from evil.

This has been called 'The Lord's Prayer' because it is a prayer that Jesus taught. (Jesus' followers called him 'Lord'.) Christians all over the world still say this prayer, in their own language.

R51

> **Q** Do you know any other written prayers? How are they similar? How are they different?

> **Q** What would you say if you were talking to God?

Who's important?

Jesus' journey is getting harder. His closest friends start to believe that he is the *Messiah*, God's special leader. They don't understand when he tells them that his journey will end in death. As they follow him towards *Jerusalem*, they think they know what's important for Jesus...

MATTHEW 19:13-15

13 Some people brought their children to Jesus, so that he could place his hands on them and pray for them. His disciples told the people to stop bothering him. **14** But Jesus said, "Let the children come to me, and don't try to stop them! People who are like these children belong to God's **kingdom**." **15** After Jesus had placed his hands on the children, he left.

→ R 74

> **Q** What does Jesus think about children?

Who is he?

Jesus has been on his journey for three years. Now he joins thousands of others making their way to the city for the Jewish *Passover* festival. He's been to *Jerusalem* before, but this time it's different. People want answers to their questions about Jesus – who is he?

MATTHEW 21:1-11

1 When Jesus and his **disciples** came near **Jerusalem**, he went to Bethphage on the Mount of Olives and sent two of them on ahead. **2** He told them, "Go into the next village, where you will at once find a donkey and her colt. Untie the two donkeys and bring them to me. **3** It anyone asks why you are doing that, just say, '**The Lord** needs them.' Straight away he will let you have the donkeys."

4 So God's promise came true, just as the **prophet** had said,

5 "Announce to the people of Jerusalem: 'Your king is coming to you! He is humble and rides on a donkey. He comes on the colt of a donkey.'"

> **Verse 5** The prophet Zechariah spoke these words about a future leader, the **Messiah**.

6 The disciples left and did what Jesus had told them to do. **7** They brought the donkey and its colt and laid some clothes on their backs. Then Jesus got on.
8 Many people spread clothes in the road, while others put down branches which they had cut from trees. **9** Some people walked ahead of Jesus and others followed behind. They were all shouting,

"Hooray for the **Son of David**! God bless the one who comes in the name of the Lord. Hooray for God in heaven above!"

10 When Jesus came to Jerusalem, everyone in the city was excited and asked, "Who can this be?"

11 The crowd answered, "This is Jesus, the prophet from Nazareth in Galilee."

> **Q** Have you ever been part of a crowd? Can you imagine being in this crowd, welcoming Jesus?

The three servants

Jesus knows that the leaders don't agree with his answers and don't believe that God has sent him. His life is in danger, so he tells stories. He wants everyone to understand about God's kingdom now and in the future.

For more stories Jesus told R75, R76, R77

MATTHEW 25:14–30

14 The kingdom is also like what happened when a man went away and put his three servants in charge of all he owned. **15** The man knew what each servant could do. So he handed five thousand coins to the first servant, two thousand to the second, and one thousand to the third. Then he left the country.

16 As soon as the man had gone, the servant with the five thousand coins used them to earn five thousand more. **17** The servant who had two thousand coins did the same with his money and earned two thousand more. **18** But the servant with one thousand coins dug a hole and hid his master's money in the ground.

19 Some time later the master of those servants returned. He called them in and asked what they had done with his money. **20** The servant who had been given five thousand coins brought them in with the five thousand that he had earned. He said, "Sir, you gave me five thousand coins, and I have earned five thousand more."

21 "Wonderful!" his master replied. "You are a good and faithful servant. I left you in charge of only a little, but now I will put you in charge of much more. Come and share in my happiness!"

22 Next, the servant who had been given two thousand coins came in and said, "Sir, you gave me two thousand coins, and I have earned two thousand more."

23 "Wonderful!" his master replied. "You are a good and faithful servant. I left you in charge of only a little, but now I will put you in charge of much more. Come and share in my happiness!"

24 The servant who had been given one thousand coins then came in and said, "Sir, I know that you are hard to get along with. You harvest what you don't plant and gather crops where you haven't scattered seed. **25** I was frightened and went out and hid your money in the ground. Here is every single coin!"

26 The master of the servant told him, "You are lazy and good-for-nothing! You know that I harvest what I don't plant and gather crops where I haven't scattered seed. **27** You could have at least put my money in the bank, so that I could have earned interest on it."

28 Then the master said, "Now your money will be taken away and given to the servant with ten thousand coins! **29** Everyone who has something will be given more, and they will have more than enough. But everything will be taken from those who don't have anything. **30** You are a worthless servant, and you will be thrown out into the dark where people will cry and grit their teeth in pain."

> **Q** What parts of the story does Jesus repeat? What other stories do you know which use repetition?

> **Q** Which character would you like to be in this story?

The meal

Jesus and his friends have come to Jerusalem for the *Passover*. **As Jesus' enemies are plotting against him, they have to meet in a secret place.**

MATTHEW 26:17–30

17 On the first day of the Festival of Thin Bread, Jesus' **disciples** came to him and asked, "Where do you want us to prepare the **Passover** meal?"

18 Jesus told them to go to a certain man in the city and tell him, "Our teacher says, 'My time has come! I want to eat the Passover meal with my disciples in your home.'"

19 They did as Jesus told them and prepared the meal.

20–21 When Jesus was eating with his twelve disciples that evening, he said, "One of you will hand me over to my enemies."

22 The disciples were very sad, and each one said to Jesus, "Lord, you can't mean me!"

23 He answered, "One of you men who has eaten with me from this dish will betray me. **24** The **Son of Man** will die, as the **Scriptures** say. But it's going to be

R17

R19
R20
R21

R96

Passover At Passover, Jewish people remember how God rescued their ancestors from Egypt. At one part of the meal the leader holds up the large piece of bread without yeast (thin bread) and breaks it. Later the leader holds up a cup of wine and passes it round for them to drink.

terrible for the one who betrays me! That man would be better off if he had never been born."

25 Judas said, "Teacher, surely you don't mean me!"

"That's what you say!" Jesus replied. But later, Judas did betray him.

26 During the meal Jesus took some bread in his hands. He blessed the bread and broke it. Then he gave it to his disciples and said, "Take this and eat it. This is my body."

27 Jesus picked up a cup of wine and gave thanks to God. He then gave it to his disciples and said, "Take this and drink it. **28** This is my blood, and with it God makes his agreement with you. It will be poured out, so that many people will have their sins forgiven. **29** From now on I am not going to drink any wine, until I drink new wine with you in my **Father's** kingdom." **30** Then they sang a hymn and went out to the Mount of Olives.

God made an old agreement or covenant with his people when he set them free from being slaves in Egypt. He agreed to go on loving them and they had to keep his laws. If they disobeyed, they asked God to forgive them, by killing an animal. When the animal died, it was as if the sin was gone too. Jesus tells his friends about a new agreement. Instead of an animal dying, Jesus himself was going to die – no more animals to be killed if people wanted their sins forgiven.

R19, R20, R21, R41, R45

The food and cups of wine at the Passover meal are symbols of how God set people free in Moses' time. Jesus now uses bread and wine as symbols of the new agreement. He wants his friends to remember that his death will set them free.

R96

Q Do you ever have a meal to remember a big occasion? Do you say (or sing) any special words?

Q What do you think Jesus meant when he talked about his body (verse 26) and blood (verse 28)?

Not what I want

It's night-time. Jesus has shared the Passover meal with his friends. He has told his friends that he will die. Now he goes to a quiet place to talk to God.

R21

MATTHEW 26:36–46

36 Jesus went with his **disciples** to a place called **Gethsemane**. When they got there, he told them, "Sit here while I go over there and pray."

37 Jesus took along Peter and the two brothers, James and John. He was very sad and troubled, **38** and he said to them, "I am so sad that I feel as if I am dying. Stay here and keep awake with me."

39 Jesus walked on a little way. Then he knelt with his face to the ground and prayed, "My **Father**, if it is possible, don't make me suffer by making me drink from this cup. But do what you want, and not what I want."

40 He came back and found his disciples sleeping. So he said to Peter, "Can't any of you stay awake with me for just one hour? **41** Stay awake and pray that you won't be tested. You want to do what is right, but you are weak."

42 Again Jesus went to pray and said, "My Father, if there is no other way, and I must suffer, I will still do what you want."

43 Jesus came back and found them sleeping again. They simply could not keep their eyes open. **44** He left them and prayed the same prayer once more.

45 Finally, Jesus returned to his disciples and said, "Are you still sleeping and resting? The time has come for the **Son of Man** to be handed over to sinners. **46** Get up! Let's go. The one who will betray me is already here."

Q Why did Jesus ask his friends to come with him?

Q Why did Jesus have to do what his Father wanted?

On trial

Judas leads an armed gang to arrest Jesus. They take Jesus to the Jewish High Priest, who questions him. The priest and his council become angry at Jesus' answers. They believe he is committing blasphemy, saying that he is God. The penalty is death. They can't kill Jesus themselves so they hand him to the Romans. The Roman governor, Pontius Pilate, puts Jesus on trial.

MATTHEW 27:15–26

15 During Passover the governor always freed a prisoner chosen by the people. **16** At that time a well-known terrorist named Jesus Barabbas was in jail. **17** So when the crowd came together, Pilate asked them, "Which prisoner do you want me to set free? Do you want Jesus Barabbas or Jesus who is called the **Messiah**?" **18** Pilate knew that the leaders had brought Jesus to him because they were jealous.

19 While Pilate was judging the case, his wife sent him a message. It said, "Don't have anything to do with that innocent man. I have had nightmares because of him."

20 But the chief priests and the leaders convinced the crowds to ask for Barabbas to be set free and for Jesus to be killed. **21** Pilate asked the crowd again, "Which of these two men do you want me to set free?"

"Barabbas!" they replied.

22 Pilate asked them, "What am I to do with Jesus, who is called the Messiah?"

They all yelled, "Nail him to a cross!

23 Pilate answered, "But what crime has he done?"

"Nail him to a cross!" they yelled even louder.

Judas
R56

24 Pilate saw that there was nothing he could do and that the people were starting to riot. So he took some water and washed his hands in front of them and said, "I won't have anything to do with killing this man. You are the ones doing it!"

25 Everyone answered, "We and our own families will take the blame for his death!"

26 Pilate set Barabbas free. Then he ordered his soldiers to beat Jesus with a whip and nail him to a cross.

> **Q** Would you say the Roman governor Pilate was a weak or strong leader?

> **Q** How might you have felt if you had been Barabbas?

What you want...

The story continues...

MATTHEW 27:27–32

27 The governor's soldiers led Jesus into the fortress and brought together the rest of the troops. **28** They stripped off Jesus' clothes and put a scarlet robe on him. **29** They made a crown out of thorn branches and placed it on his head, and they put a stick in his right hand. The soldiers knelt down and pretended to worship him. They made fun of him and shouted, "Hey, you king of the Jews!" **30** Then they spat on him. They took the stick from him and beat him on the head with it.

31 When the soldiers had finished making fun of Jesus, they took off the robe. They put his own clothes back on him and led him off to be nailed to a cross. **32** On the way they met a man from Cyrene named Simon, and they forced him to carry Jesus' cross.

> **Q** The crowds who had welcomed Jesus in R54 are the same crowd who want to see Jesus dead. Why do you think they changed their minds?

Nailed to a cross

The story continues...

MATTHEW 27:33–44

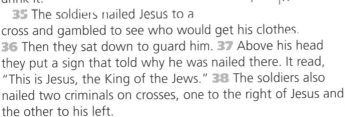

33 They came to a place named Golgotha, which means "Place of a Skull". **34** There they gave Jesus some wine mixed with a drug to ease the pain. But when Jesus tasted what it was, he refused to drink it.

35 The soldiers nailed Jesus to a cross and gambled to see who would get his clothes. **36** Then they sat down to guard him. **37** Above his head they put a sign that told why he was nailed there. It read, "This is Jesus, the King of the Jews." **38** The soldiers also nailed two criminals on crosses, one to the right of Jesus and the other to his left.

39 People who passed by said terrible things about Jesus. They shook their heads and **40** shouted, "So you're the one who claimed you could tear down the temple and build it again in three days! If you are God's Son, save yourself and come down from the cross!"

41 The chief **priests**, the leaders, and the teachers of the **Law of Moses** also made fun of Jesus. They said, **42** "He saved others, but he can't save himself. If he is the king of Israel, he should come down from the cross! Then we will believe him. **43** He trusted God, so let God save him, if he wants to. He even said he was God's Son." **44** The two criminals also said cruel things to Jesus.

The Roman soldiers nailed Jesus to a wooden cross because this was their usual death sentence for criminals. They called it crucifixion. Christians remember Jesus' crucifixion on Good Friday.

The story goes on…Read what happens in R86.

R58

Q Who in the story in R59 and R60 gives any help to Jesus?

Q Why was Jesus killed like a criminal?

Matthew 28:1–10

R61 **Alive!**

Jesus dies on Friday afternoon. A rich *disciple* takes his body to bury it in a *tomb* and rolls a large stone across the opening. On Saturday (the Sabbath) everyone has to rest. On Sunday morning, Jesus' mum and his friend Mary set out to do the last thing they can for Jesus – give him a proper burial.

MATTHEW 28:1–10

1 The **Sabbath** was over, and it was almost daybreak on Sunday when **Mary Magdalene** and the other Mary went to see the **tomb**. **2** Suddenly a strong earthquake struck, and the Lord's **angel** came down from heaven. He rolled away the stone and sat on it. **3** The angel looked as bright as lightning, and his clothes were white as snow. **4** The guards shook from fear and fell down, as though they were dead.

5 The angel said to the women, "Don't be afraid! I know you are looking for Jesus, who was nailed to a cross. **6** He isn't here! God has raised him to life, just as Jesus said he would.

Come, see the place where his body was lying. **7** Now hurry! Tell his **disciples** that he has been raised to life and is on his way to **Galilee**. Go there, and you will see him. That is what I came to tell you."

8 The women were frightened and yet very happy, as they hurried from the tomb and ran to tell his disciples.
9 Suddenly Jesus met them and greeted them. They went near him, held on to his feet, and **worshipped** him.
10 Then Jesus said, "Don't be afraid! Tell my followers to go to Galilee. They will see me there."

Q What was the women's message and who told them to say it?

Q On what day do Christians celebrate Jesus' resurrection – coming back to life?

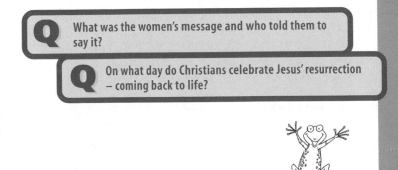

Go!

Jesus is alive again. In the next 40 days he meets his disciples many times. Matthew only writes about one of these times, and finishes his gospel with these words:

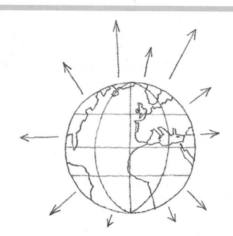

MATTHEW 28:16–20

16 Jesus' eleven **disciples** went to a mountain in **Galilee**, where Jesus had told them to meet him. **17** They saw him and **worshipped** him, but some of them doubted.
18 Jesus came to them and said:

I have been given all authority in heaven and on earth!
19 Go to the people of all nations and make them my disciples. **Baptize** them in the name of the Father, the Son, and the Holy Spirit, **20** and teach them to do everything I have told you. I will be with you always, even until the end of the world.

Q Why do you think Matthew specially remembered this time when Jesus met him and the other disciples?

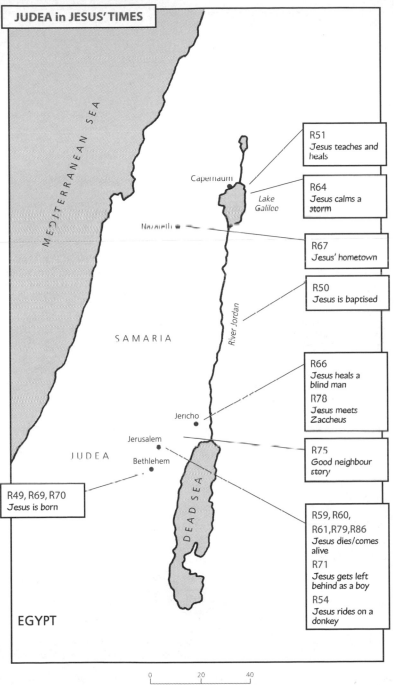

JUDEA in JESUS' TIMES

MEDITERRANEAN SEA

Capernaum

Lake Galilee

Nazareth

River Jordan

SAMARIA

Jericho

Jerusalem

JUDEA

Bethlehem

DEAD SEA

EGYPT

R51
Jesus teaches and heals

R64
Jesus calms a storm

R67
Jesus' hometown

R50
Jesus is baptised

R66
Jesus heals a blind man

R78
Jesus meets Zaccheus

R75
Good neighbour story

R49, R69, R70
Jesus is born

R59, R60, R61, R79, R86
Jesus dies/comes alive

R71
Jesus gets left behind as a boy

R54
Jesus rides on a donkey

0   20   40
Kilometres

Jesus

⭐ Star factor

★ Saviour of the world

Key Bible verse

The Word became a human being and lived here with us. *John 1:14* (R80)

God loved the people of the world so much that he gave his only Son, so that everyone who has faith in him will have eternal life and never really die. *John 3:16* (R81)

Jesus claimed to be all these things – light, bread, gate and shepherd

---

Find out who said:

'This is my own dear Son and I am pleased with him.'

'You are the Messiah sent from God.'

'In the name of Jesus Christ of Nazareth, get up and start walking.'

R50 (A voice from heaven), R74 (Peter), R90 (Peter)

Mary — 1st Century

Jesus — 1st Century

What the Bible says about Jesus

★ He lived as a human being, was hungry, happy, sad, fell asleep (R48, R57, R63, R64, R71)

★ His brother James became the leader of the church in Jerusalem

★ He spent time with the hungry, poor or those undervalued by others (like children) (R53, R66, R78)

★ He died on a wooden cross (the way Romans killed criminals) (R60, R79, R86)

★ He came back to life after two days, and for the next 40 days saw many of his followers (R61,R62)

★ He returned to heaven. Ten days later his followers received power to continue his work (R88,R89)

★ Millions more people followed him after he had gone back to heaven

What others said about Jesus in the Bible

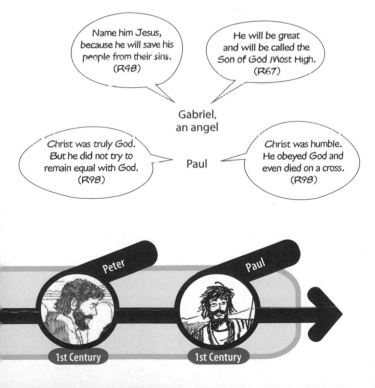

Name him Jesus, because he will save his people from their sins. (R48)

He will be great and will be called the Son of God Most High. (R67)

Gabriel, an angel

Christ was truly God. But he did not try to remain equal with God. (R98)

Paul

Christ was humble. He obeyed God and even died on a cross. (R98)

Peter

Paul

1st Century

1st Century

Into the desert

Just after Jesus is baptised he goes away by himself.

MARK 1:12–13

12 Straightaway God's Spirit made Jesus go into the desert.
13 He stayed there for forty days while Satan tested him.
Jesus was with the wild animals, but angels took care of him.

R50

> **Q** Why do you think Jesus needed to go into the desert for such a long time?

The storm

Jesus has been sitting in a boat and talking to a large crowd on the shore. Storms start quickly on Lake Galilee. Jesus' disciples know this but even they aren't prepared for what happens next...

MARK 4:35–41

35 That evening, Jesus said to his disciples, "Let's cross to the east side." **36** So they left the crowd, and his disciples started across the lake with him in the boat. Some other boats followed along. **37** Suddenly a storm struck the lake. Waves started splashing into the boat, and it was about to sink.

38 Jesus was in the back of the boat with his head on a pillow, and he was asleep. His disciples woke him and said, "Teacher, don't you care that we're about to drown?"

39 Jesus got up and ordered the wind and the waves to be

Map page 121

quiet. The wind stopped, and everything was calm.

10 Jesus asked his disciples, "Why were you afraid? Don't you have any faith?"

41 Now they were more afraid than ever and said to each other, "Who is this? Even the wind and the waves obey him!"

> **Q** Why were the disciples more afraid after Jesus stopped the storm?

> **Q** What makes you frightened? Who or what helps you not to be afraid?

Life and health

Jesus and his disciples are using boats to reach people in remote places around Lake Galilee. Now they head back to Capernaum.

MARK 5:21–24,35–43

21 Once again Jesus got into the boat and crossed Lake Galilee. Then as he stood on the shore, a large crowd gathered around him. **22** The person in charge of the Jewish meeting place was also there. His name was Jairus, and when he saw Jesus, he went over to him. He knelt at Jesus' feet **23** and started begging him for help. He said, "My daughter is about to die! Please come and touch her, so she will get well and live." **24** Jesus went with Jairus. Many people followed along and kept crowding around…

35 While Jesus was still speaking, some men came from Jairus' home and said, "Your daughter has died! Why bother the teacher any more?"

36 Jesus heard what they said, and he said to Jairus, "Don't worry. Just have faith!"

37 Jesus did not let anyone go with him except Peter and the two brothers, James and John. **38** They went home with Jairus and saw the people crying and making a lot of noise. **39** Then Jesus went inside and said to them, "Why are you crying and carrying on like this? The child isn't dead. She is just asleep." **40** But the people laughed at him.

After Jesus had sent them all out of the house, he took the girl's father and mother and his three disciples and went to where she was. **41–42** He took the twelve-year-old girl by the hand and said, "Talitha, koum!" which means, "Little girl, get up!" The girl got straight up and started walking around.

Everyone was greatly surprised. **43** But Jesus ordered them not to tell anyone what had happened. Then he said, "Give her something to eat."

Q What difference did Jesus make to the girl's life?

I want to see!

Jesus is now on his way to *Jerusalem* and passes through Jericho.

MARK 10:46–52

46 Jesus and his disciples went to Jericho. And as they were leaving, they were followed by a large crowd. A blind beggar called Bartimaeus son of Timaeus was sitting beside the road. **47** When he heard that it was Jesus from Nazareth, he shouted, "Jesus, **Son of David**, have pity on me!" **48** Many people told the man to stop, but he shouted even louder, "Son of David, have pity on me!"

49 Jesus stopped and said, "Call him over!" They called out to the blind man and said, "Don't be afraid! Come on! He is calling for you." **50** The man threw off his coat as he jumped up and ran to Jesus.

51 Jesus asked, "What do you want me to do for you?" The blind man answered, "Master, I want to see!"

52 Jesus told him, "You may go. Your eyes are healed because of your faith." Straight away the man could see, and he went down the road with Jesus.

R78

Map page 121

Names of Jesus
Son of David – people called Jesus by this name, because he was like King David.

Q What did Bartimaeus have that was important? (verse 52)

R67

The angel's message

Luke starts his gospel at the time of King Herod. Jewish people are waiting for their *Messiah*. Gabriel, an *angel*, gives a message to an old *priest*, Zechariah. Though Zechariah's wife Elizabeth is too old to have children, the angel says that they will have their first son, John. Six months later, Gabriel has a message for Elizabeth's young cousin, Mary.

LUKE 1:26-38

26 God sent the angel Gabriel to the town of Nazareth in **Galilee 27** with a message for a virgin named Mary. She was engaged to Joseph from the family of **King David**.

28 The angel greeted Mary and said, "You are truly blessed! **The Lord** is with you."

29 Mary was confused by the angel's words and wondered what they meant. **30** Then the angel told Mary, "Don't be afraid! God is pleased with you, **31** and you will have a son. His name will be Jesus. **32** He will be great and will be called the Son of God Most High. The Lord God will make him king, as his ancestor David was. **33** He will rule the people of Israel for ever, and his kingdom will never end."

34 Mary asked the angel, "How can this happen? I am not married!"

35 The angel answered, "The **Holy Spirit** will come down to you, and God's power will come over you. So your child will be called the holy Son of God. **36** Your relative Elizabeth

Gabriel tells Mary about her baby. But Mary has a BIG question. She isn't married and has never had sex – how can she have a baby?
Luke is a doctor. He knows that other people will ask the same question. So he starts his gospel by writing about another 'impossible' baby. Elizabeth's experience helps Mary to believe the angel. The Holy Spirit, the power of God, will make it possible.

is also going to have a son, even though she is old. No one thought she could ever have a baby, but in three months she will have a son. **37** Nothing is impossible for God!"

38 Mary said, "I am the Lord's servant! Let it happen as you have said." And the angel left her.

Q Mary is engaged to Joseph. Can you imagine how Mary tells Joseph about the angel's visit? How will Joseph react?

R48

Q What does the future hold for Mary's baby?

Mary's song

After Gabriel's visit, Mary travels from Galilee to Judea to see her cousin Elizabeth. As soon as Mary enters, the Holy Spirit helps Elizabeth to realise that Mary's baby will be very special. Mary replies...

LUKE 1:46–56
46 Mary said:

With all my heart I praise the Lord,
47 and I am glad because of God my **Saviour**.
48 He cares for me, his humble servant. From now on, all people will say God has blessed me.
49 God All-Powerful has done great things for me, and his name is **holy**.
50 He always shows mercy to everyone who worships him.
51 The Lord has used his powerful arm to scatter those who are proud.

52 He drags strong rulers from their thrones and puts humble people in places of power.

53 God gives the hungry good things to eat, and sends the rich away with nothing.

54 He helps his servant Israel and is always merciful to his people.

Sometimes Mary's song is called by its first word in **Latin** – Magnificat.

55 The Lord made this promise to our ancestors, to Abraham and his family for ever!

56 Mary stayed with Elizabeth about three months. Then she went back home.

R6, R40, R43, R46

Q Think of something exciting that has happened that you would want to tell people about. Could you say it with a song, a picture or a poem?

Q Mary's words show that she knew the Jewish **scriptures** about Abraham (R6) and the **prophets**. Do you know people who know their holy book well? How do they learn?

R69

Luke 2:1–7

How Jesus was born

NT

The lands of *Judea* and *Galilee* are under Roman control. Joseph and Mary have to travel about 100km so that the Romans can keep their tax records up to date.

R48, R67

LUKE 2:1–7

1 About that time Emperor Augustus gave orders for the names of all the people to be listed in record books. **2** These first records were made when Quirinius was governor of Syria.

3 Everyone had to go to their own home town to be listed. **4** So Joseph had to leave Nazareth in Galilee and go to **Bethlehem** in Judea. Long ago Bethlehem had been **King David's** home town, and Joseph went there because he was from David's family.

5 Mary was engaged to Joseph and travelled with him to Bethlehem. She was soon going to have a baby, **6** and while they were there, **7** she gave birth to her firstborn son. She dressed him in baby clothes and laid him on a bed of hay, because there was no room for them in the inn.

> **Q** Have you ever seen or acted the birth of Jesus in a nativity play? What was the same as Luke's account? What was different?

> **Q** If you had to return to your grandparents' village, town or country, where would you go?

Who saw Jesus first?

The Romans have ordered all Jewish people to go back to their ancestor's home town. In Bethlehem, a baby boy is born and placed on a bed of hay. Meanwhile, outside the town...

LUKE 2:8–20
8 That night in the fields near Bethlehem some shepherds were guarding their sheep. **9** All at once an **angel** came

down to them from the Lord, and the brightness of the Lord's glory flashed around them. The shepherds were frightened. **10** But the angel said, "Don't be afraid! I have good news for you, which will make everyone happy. **11** This very day in **King David's** home town a **Saviour** was born for you. He is **Christ the Lord**. **12** You will know who he is, because you will find him dressed in baby clothes and lying on a bed of hay."

13 Suddenly many other angels came down from heaven and joined in praising God. They said:

14 "Praise God in heaven! Peace on earth to everyone who pleases God."

15 After the angels had left and gone back to heaven, the shepherds said to each other, "Let's go to Bethlehem and see what the Lord has told us about." **16** They hurried off and found Mary and Joseph, and they saw the baby lying on a bed of hay.

17 When the shepherds saw Jesus, they told his parents what the angel had said about him. **18** Everyone listened and was surprised. **19** But Mary kept thinking about all this and wondering what it meant.

20 As the shepherds returned to their sheep, they were praising God and saying wonderful things about him. Everything they had seen and heard was just as the angel had said.

← For more visitors to Jesus R49

Q First of all, why were the shepherds afraid? Why were they so happy at the end?

Lost?

When Jesus is still a baby, Joseph and Mary take him to the *temple* in *Jerusalem*. An old man (Simeon) prays for him, and an old woman (Anna) says that God has a special plan for the baby. Luke records one other event that happened when Jesus was young:

LUKE 2:40–52

40 The child Jesus grew. He became strong and wise, and God blessed him. **41** Every year Jesus' parents went to Jerusalem for **Passover**. **42** And when Jesus was twelve years old, they all went there as usual for the celebration. **43** After Passover his parents left, but they did not know that Jesus had stayed on in the city. **44** They thought he was travelling with some other people, and they went a whole day before they started looking for him. **45** When they could not find him with their relatives and friends, they went back to Jerusalem and started looking for him there.

> **Verse 42** In their thirteenth year, Jewish boys have a test of their knowledge of Scripture. They can then take their place as men in the Jewish community.

46 Three days later they found Jesus sitting in the temple, listening to the teachers and asking them questions. **47** Everyone who heard him was surprised at how much he knew and at the answers he gave.

48 When his parents found him, they were amazed. His mother said, "Son, why have you done this to us? Your father and I have been very worried, and we have been searching for you!"

49 Jesus answered, "Why did you have to look for me? Didn't you know that I would be in my **Father's** house?" **50** But they did not understand what he meant.

51 Jesus went back to Nazareth with his parents and obeyed them. His mother kept on thinking about all that had happened.

52 Jesus became wise, and he grew strong. God was pleased with him and so were the people.

> **Q** What do you notice about Jesus' attitude to his parents and also to the teachers at the temple?

R72 **Fishing**

It's the fifteenth year of the Roman emperor, Tiberius. Lake Galilee is a popular place. The lake provides work (fishing, boat-building) and a way of travelling. New ideas or stories spread quickly to other areas. Jesus comes to the lake to start teaching a new message from God.

LUKE 5:1–11

1 Jesus was standing on the shore of Lake **Gennesaret**, teaching the people as they crowded around him to hear God's message. **2** Near the shore he saw two boats left there by some fishermen who had gone to wash their nets. **3** Jesus got into the boat that belonged to Simon and asked him to row it out a little way from the shore. Then Jesus sat down in the boat to teach the crowd.

4 When Jesus had finished speaking, he told Simon, "Row

the boat out into the deep water and let your nets down to catch some fish."

5 "Master," Simon answered, "we have worked hard all night long and have not caught a thing. But if you tell me to, I will let the nets down." **6** They did it and caught so many fish that their nets began ripping apart. **7** Then they signalled for their partners in the other boat to come and help them. The men came, and together they filled the two boats so full that they both began to sink.

Peter–IP8, page 136

8 When Simon Peter saw this happen, he knelt down in front of Jesus and said, "Lord, don't come near me! I am a **sinner**." **9** Peter and everyone with him were completely surprised at all the fish they had caught. **10** His partners James and John, the sons of Zebedee, were surprised too.

> **Verse 8** Simon the fisherman was given a new name, Peter, which means the rock. In other places in *Into the Bible* he is just called Peter.

Jesus told Simon, "Don't be afraid! From now on you will bring in people instead of fish." **11** The men pulled their boats up on the shore. Then they left everything and went with Jesus.

Q Who would you be prepared to follow? Why?

Peter

Also known as Simon

⭐ Star factor

★ (Like David) put his heart and soul into everything he did

Key Bible verse

So I will call you Peter, which means "a rock". On this rock I will build my church, and death itself will not have any power over it.
Matthew 16:18

Big events in Peter's life

Fishiest	Caught a boatful of fish after Jesus told him what to do (R72)
Riskiest	Left his family with the boatful of fish, and followed Jesus (R72)
Wettest	Walked on water towards Jesus – and sank!
Weakest	Told strangers that he did not know Jesus (R85)
Humblest	Faced Jesus afterwards (Jesus forgave him) (R87)
Boldest	Told thousands of strangers how they could follow Jesus

Mary — 1st Century

Jesus — 1st Century

C E

What the Bible says about Peter

More about Peter in the Bible

Escapes from prison:
Acts 12:6–19

Sees Jesus as he really is:
Matthew 17:1–8

★ He was married – Jesus healed his wife's mum, who lived in the same house

★ He was one of Jesus' closest friends

★ His name changed, from Simon to Peter, which means 'a rock'

★ He became leader of the disciples after Jesus went back to heaven (R89, R90)

★ He was filled with the Holy Spirit to help him speak God's words (R89)

Everyday life in Capernaum, 30 CE

Peter and his neighbours spoke Aramaic. They would read and write in Greek.

The Jewish Scriptures had been translated into Greek.

They were ruled by the Romans and had to pay them taxes.

They had their own religious leaders and travelled to Jerusalem for big festivals.

Their ancestors won a victory against the Greeks. They still hoped for a leader to rescue them from the Romans.

Peter

Paul

1st Century

1st Century

R73

A different way to live

Like Matthew, Luke writes down some of Jesus' words about living in God's way – even when other people try to make it difficult.

R51,R52

R79

LUKE 6:27–31,35–36

27 This is what I say to all who will listen to me:

Love your enemies, and be good to everyone who hates you. **28** Ask God to bless anyone who curses you, and pray for everyone who is cruel to you. **29** If someone slaps you on one cheek, don't stop that person from slapping you on the other cheek. If someone wants to take your coat, don't try and keep back your shirt. **30** Give to everyone who asks and don't ask people to return what they have taken from you. **31** Treat others just as you want to be treated....

Jesus didn't just talk about getting on with enemies – he showed it in the way he treated the people who arrested and killed him.

35 But love your enemies and be good to them. Lend without expecting to be paid back. Then you will get a great reward, and you will be the true children of God in heaven. He is good even to people who are unthankful and cruel. **36** Have pity on others, just as your **Father** has pity on you.

Verse 36 Jesus wanted his hearers to know that God had already done something to make this way of life possible.

Q Which of these 'ways to live' would be easy to follow? Which would be most difficult? Why?

Who am I?

Jesus has been teaching and healing. He has just fed over 5000 people and knows that people are making up their minds about him. So he asks his friends what they think.

LUKE 9:18–27

18 When Jesus was alone praying, his **disciples** came to him, and he asked them, "What do people say about me?"

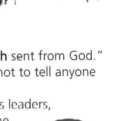

19 They answered, "Some say that you are **John the Baptist** or Elijah or a **prophet** from long ago who has come back to life."

20 Jesus then asked them, "But who do you say I am?"

Peter answered, "You are the **Messiah** sent from God."

21 Jesus strictly warned his disciples not to tell anyone about this.

22 Jesus told his disciples, "The nation's leaders, the chief **priests**, and the teachers of the **Law of Moses** will make the **Son of Man** suffer terribly. They will reject him and kill him, but three days later he will rise to life."

23 Then Jesus said to all the people: If any of you want to be my followers, you must forget about yourself. You must take up your cross each day and follow me. **24** If you want to save your life, you will destroy it. But if you give up your life for me, you will save it.

Messiah Each of the accounts of Jesus' life are about this question – is Jesus the **Messiah**?
Christ – wasn't Jesus' surname! It's the Greek word for **Messiah**. Later on, people gave this name to Jesus.

25 What will you gain, if you own the whole world but destroy yourself or waste your life? **26** If you are ashamed of me and my message, the Son of Man will be ashamed of you when he comes in his glory and in the glory of his Father and the holy angels. **27** You can be sure that some of the people standing here will not die before they see God's kingdom.

> **Q** Why do you think the disciples carried on following Jesus, even though he told them his way would be difficult? What might you have done if you had been one of his followers?

R75 A good neighbour

Jesus has sent 72 of his followers to talk about God's message. A lot of people throughout Judea and Galilee have heard about Jesus' way of following God. People now listen to Jesus' teaching rather than their Jewish leaders. So these leaders have some big questions.

LUKE 10:25–37

25 An expert in the **Law of Moses** stood up and asked Jesus a question to see what he would say. "Teacher," he asked, "what must I do to have **eternal life**?"

26 Jesus answered, "What is written in the **Scriptures**? How do you understand them?"

27 The man replied, "The Scriptures say, 'Love the Lord your God with all your heart, soul, strength, and mind.' They also say, 'Love your neighbours as much as you love yourself.'"

> **Verse 27** The expert took his answer from the Jewish **Scriptures** – find it in R22. Neighbour means any other person, wherever they live.

28 Jesus said, "You have given the right answer. If you do this, you will have **eternal** life."

29 But the man wanted to show that he knew what he was talking about. So he asked Jesus, "Who are my neighbours?"

30 Jesus replied:

As a man was going down from **Jerusalem** to Jericho, robbers attacked him and grabbed everything he had. They beat him up and ran off, leaving him half dead. **31** A **priest** happened to be going down the same road. But when he saw the man, he walked by on the other side. **32** Later a **temple** helper came to the same place. But when he saw the man who had been beaten up, he also went by on the other side. **33** A man from **Samaria** then came travelling along that road. When he saw the man, he felt sorry for him **34** and went over to him. He treated his wounds with olive oil and wine and bandaged them. Then he put him on his own donkey and took him to an inn, where he took care of him. **35** The next morning he gave the innkeeper two silver coins and said, "Please take care of the man. If you spend more than this on him, I will pay you when I return."

36 Then Jesus asked, "Which one of these three people was a real neighbour to the man who was beaten up by robbers?"

37 The teacher answered, "The one who showed pity." Jesus said, "Go and do the same!"

Map
page
121

> **Q** How would you answer the question, "Who are my neighbours?" (verse 29)?

R76 Lost and found 1

The Jewish leaders are trying to follow God. They have very strong ideas about who else could follow God as well. They can't understand why Jesus wants to share God's message with everyone – even 'bad' people!

LUKE 15:1–7

1 **Tax collectors** and **sinners** were all crowding around to listen to Jesus. **2** So the **Pharisees** and the **teachers of the Law of Moses** started grumbling, "This man is friendly with sinners. He even eats with them."

3 Then Jesus told them this story:

4 If any of you has a hundred sheep, and one of them gets lost, what will you do? Won't you leave the ninety-nine in the field and go and look for the lost sheep until you find it? **5** And when you find it, you will be so glad that you will put it on your shoulder **6** and carry it home. Then you will call in your friends and neighbours and say, "Let's celebrate! I've found my lost sheep."

7 Jesus said, "In the same way there is more happiness in heaven because of one sinner who turns to God than over ninety-nine good people who don't need to."

Q What would be in *your* story about something special that was lost and found?

Lost and found 2

R77

Jesus continues to talk to all his listeners…

LUKE 15:11–32

11 Jesus also told them another story:

Once a man had two sons. **12** The younger son said to his father, "Give me my share of the property." So the father divided his property between his two sons.

13 Not long after that, the younger son packed up everything he owned and left for a foreign country, where he wasted all his money in wild living **14** He had spent everything, when a bad famine spread through that whole land. Soon he had nothing to eat.

15 He went to work for a man in that country, and the man sent him out to take care of his pigs. **16** He would have been glad to eat what the pigs were eating, but no one gave him a thing.

> **Verse 15** Shock factor! Jewish people never ate any meat from pigs. Any contact with pigs made them 'unclean'.

17 Finally, he came to his senses and said, "My father's workers have plenty to eat, and here I am, starving to death! **18** I will go to my father and say to him, 'Father, I have sinned against God in heaven and against you. **19** I am no longer good enough to be called your son. Treat me like one of your workers.'"

20 The younger son got up and started back to his

father. But when he was still a long way off, his father saw him and felt sorry for him. He ran to his son and hugged and kissed him.

21 The son said, "Father, I have sinned against God in heaven and against you. I am no longer good enough to be called your son."

22 But his father said to the servants, "Hurry and bring the best clothes and put them on him. Give him a ring for his finger and sandals for his feet. **23** Get the best calf and prepare it, so we can eat and celebrate. **24** This son of mine was dead, but has now come back to life. He was lost and has now been found." And they began to celebrate.

25 The elder son had been out in the field. But when he came near the house, he heard the music and dancing. **26** So he called one of the servants over and asked, "What's going on here?"

27 The servant answered, "Your brother has come home safe and sound, and your father ordered us to kill the best calf." **28** The elder brother got so angry that he would not even go into the house.

His father came out and begged him to go in. **29** But he said to his father, "For years I have worked for you like a slave and have always obeyed you. But you have never even given me a little goat, so that I could give a dinner for my friends. **30** This other son of yours wasted your money on prostitutes. And now that he has come home, you ordered the best calf to be killed for a feast."

31 His father replied, "My son, you are always with me, and everything I have is yours. **32** But we should be glad and celebrate! Your brother was dead, but he is now alive. He was lost and has now been found."

Q Who was in the audience when Jesus told this story (see R76, verse 1 and 2)?

Q Which character are you most like in this story?

Lost and found 3

Jesus is on the road to Jerusalem. On the way into Jericho he heals a blind man, who joins the crowds of followers. As they enter Jericho, Jesus stops to talk to another person.

LUKE 19:1–10

1 Jesus was going through Jericho, **2** where a man named Zacchaeus lived. He was in charge of collecting taxes and was very rich. **3–4** Jesus was heading his way, and Zacchaeus wanted to see what he was like. But Zacchaeus was a short man and could not see over the crowd. So he ran ahead and climbed up into a sycamore tree.

5 When Jesus got there, he looked up and said, "Zacchaeus, hurry down! I want to stay with you today." **6** Zacchaeus hurried down and gladly welcomed Jesus.

7 Everyone who saw this started grumbling, "This man Zacchaeus is a **sinner**! And Jesus is going home to eat with him."

Verse 2
Zacchaeus, the tax man, was Jewish but worked for the Romans. He cheated people by taking too much money. Jewish leaders would say that he was disobeying God.

R66

Map
page
121

8 Later that day Zacchaeus stood up and said to the Lord, "I will give half of my property to the poor. And I will now pay back four times as much to everyone I have ever cheated."

9 Jesus said to Zacchaeus, "Today you and your family

have been saved, because you are a true son of **Abraham**.
10 The **Son of Man** came to look for and to save people
who are lost."

Q Which character in the 'two sons' story (R77) is Zacchaeus
most like?
What was important to Zacchaeus a) before he met Jesus?
b) after he met Jesus?

Q What would you be prepared to do to see someone whom
you really wanted to meet?

Lost and found 4

Like Matthew, Luke records Jesus' journey into *Jerusalem*,
where the Jewish leaders become so angry with Jesus that
they arrange for him to be killed by the Romans. As Jesus is
dying, Luke records his conversation with the two criminals.

R56–60

LUKE 23:32–43

32 Two criminals were led out to be put to death with Jesus.
33 When the soldiers came to the place called "The Skull",
they nailed Jesus to a cross. They also nailed the two
criminals to crosses, one on each side of Jesus.

34-35 Jesus said, "**Father**, forgive these people! They
don't know what they're doing."

While the crowd stood there watching Jesus, the soldiers
gambled for his clothes. The leaders insulted him by saying,
"He saved others. Now he should save himself, if he really is
God's chosen **Messiah**!"

36 The soldiers made fun of Jesus and brought him some
wine. **37** They said, "If you are the king of the Jews, save
yourself!"

38 Above him was a sign that said, "This is the King of the
Jews."

39 One of the criminals hanging there also insulted Jesus by saying, "Aren't you the Messiah? Save yourself and save us!"

40 But the other criminal told the first one off, "Don't you fear God? Aren't you getting the same punishment as this man? **41** We got what was coming to us, but he didn't do anything wrong." **42** Then he said to Jesus, "Remember me when you come into power!"

43 Jesus replied, "I promise that today you will be with me in **paradise**."

> **Q** In Luke's **gospel**, the last person Jesus speaks to is a criminal. What does Luke want to tell his readers about Jesus?

The Word

R80

John 1:1–14

This gospel may have been written by the John who was a fisherman and one of Jesus' closest friends. Although he tells the story of Jesus' life and death, his gospel is different from the other three. He uses lots of pictures to help his readers understand who Jesus is. He says that Jesus is 'light for the world', 'the true vine', 'the bread of life' (R82), 'the good shepherd' and 'the gate' (R83) and 'the way, the truth and the life' (R84).

JOHN 1:1–14

1 In the beginning was the one who is called the Word. The

Word was with God and was truly God.

2 From the very beginning the Word was with God.

3 And with this Word, God created all things. Nothing was made without the Word. Everything that was created **4** received its life from him, and his life gave light to everyone.

5 The light keeps shining in the dark, and darkness has never put it out.

6 God sent a man named John, **7** who came to tell about the light and to lead all people to have faith.

8 John wasn't that light. He came only to tell about the light.

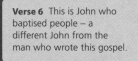

Verse 6 This is John who baptised people – a different John from the man who wrote this gospel.

9 The true light that shines on everyone was coming into the world.

10 The Word was in the world, but no one knew him, though God had made the world with his Word.

11 He came into his own world, but his own nation did not welcome him.

12 Yet some people accepted him and put their faith in him. So he gave them the right to be the children of God.

13 They were not God's children by nature or because of any human desires. God himself was the one who made them his children.

14 The Word became a human being and lived here with us. We saw his true glory, the glory of the only Son of the **Father**. From him all the kindness and all the truth of God have come down to us.

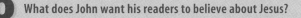

Q Read the very first words of the Bible – in R1. Read the start of John's writing. What do you notice?

Q What does John want his readers to believe about Jesus?

Late night questions

John the Baptist realises that Jesus is the one that God wants people to follow. He sends his own followers to talk to Jesus. One of them is Andrew, who tells his brother Peter, "We have found the *Messiah*". Soon other people start following Jesus, or asking questions such as Nicodemus who does not want anyone to know why he is seeing Jesus.

Peter –
IP8
Page 136

JOHN 3:1–8,16–17

1 There was a man named Nicodemus who was a **Pharisee** and a Jewish leader. **2** One night he went to Jesus and said, "Sir, we know that God has sent you to teach us. You could not perform these **miracles**, unless God were with you."

3 Jesus replied, "I tell you for certain that you must be born from above before you can see **God's kingdom**!"

4 Nicodemus asked, "How can a grown man ever be born a second time?"

5 Jesus answered:

I tell you for certain that before you can get into God's **kingdom**, you must be born not only by water, but by the **Spirit**. **6** Humans give life to their children. Yet only God's Spirit can change you into a child of God. **7** Don't be

149

surprised when I say that you must be born from above. **8** Only God's Spirit gives new life. The Spirit is like the wind that blows wherever it wants to. You can hear the wind, but you don't know where it comes from or where it is going…

Verse 5 Jesus is saying that as well as being **baptised** as a sign that they want to change, his followers also need the Holy Spirit who will help them to change.

16 God loved the people of this world so much that he gave his only Son, so that everyone who has faith in him will have eternal life and never really die. **17** God did not send his Son into the world to condemn its people. He sent him to save them!

The story continues…

Nicodemus may have come to Jesus at night because he is afraid of being seen by other Pharisees, who didn't agree with Jesus' teaching. John doesn't tell his readers straight away what Nicodemus thinks about Jesus. But later, Nicodemus speaks up for Jesus with the Jewish authorities – and he helps to bury Jesus' body.

Why did Jesus come? For many Christians, verse 16 answers this question. It is about God's love, Jesus, faith and **eternal** life. John is explaining that when people trust (have faith), they don't have to die because of the bad things they've done, but have the kind of life that God planned at the start (R2).

Q What does John want his readers to understand about Jesus? What does he want them to understand about themselves?

Enough for everyone

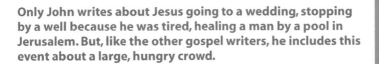

Only John writes about Jesus going to a wedding, stopping by a well because he was tired, healing a man by a pool in Jerusalem. But, like the other gospel writers, he includes this event about a large, hungry crowd.

JOHN 6:1–13

Characters:

Jesus
John *(the narrator)*
Philip *(a disciple)*
Andrew *(a disciple and brother of Simon Peter)*

John (narrator): Jesus crossed Lake Galilee, which was also known as Lake Tiberias. **2** A large crowd had seen him perform miracles to heal the sick, and those people went with him. **3–4** It was almost time for the Jewish festival of **Passover**, and Jesus went up on a mountain with us and sat down. **5** When Jesus saw the large crowd coming towards him, he asked Philip,

Jesus: Where will we get enough food to feed all these people?
John: He said this to test Philip, since he already knew what he was going to do.
Philip: Don't you know that it would take almost a year's wages just to buy only a little bread for each of these people?
Andrew: There is a boy here who has

> **Verse 10** How many? At that time, only the men were counted. The whole crowd would have included many more women and children. It could have been over 10,000 people.

five small loaves of barley bread and two fish. But what good is that with all these people?

John: The ground was covered with grass, and Jesus told his disciples,

The boy's picnic was the usual sort of food that people ate.

Jesus: Make everyone sit down.

John: About five thousand men were in the crowd. Jesus took the bread in his hands and gave thanks to God. Then he passed the bread to the people, and he did the same with the fish, until everyone had plenty to eat. The people ate all they wanted, and Jesus told his disciples,

Jesus: Gather up the leftovers, so that nothing will be wasted.

John: The disciples gathered them up and filled twelve large baskets with what was left over from the five barley loaves.

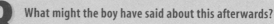

Q Why was there so much food left over?

Q What might the boy have said about this afterwards?

JOHN 6: 32–37

32 Jesus then told them, "I tell you for certain that Moses wasn't the one who gave you bread from heaven. My **Father** is the one who gives you the true bread from heaven.
33 And the bread that God gives is the one who came down from heaven to give life to the world."

34 The people said, "Lord, give us this bread and don't ever stop!"

35 Jesus replied,

I am the bread that gives life! No one who comes to me will ever be hungry. No one who has faith in me will ever be thirsty. **36** I have told you already that you have seen me and still do not have faith in me. **37** Everything and everyone that the Father has given me will come to me, and I won't turn any of them away.

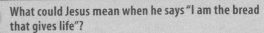

Q What could Jesus mean when he says "I am the bread that gives life"?

Q What promises does Jesus make?

I am...

People of Jesus' time would see shepherds keeping their sheep safe from wolves or bears. They knew that the shepherd would bring his flock into a sheep pen at night, and sleep across the opening. They knew that their Scriptures told of the Jewish people being sheep, with their leaders (or God himself) as shepherds.

When Jesus wants to tell people what kind of a leader he is, he talks about...

JOHN 10:6-15

6 Jesus told the people this story. But they did not understand what he was talking about. **7** Jesus said:

I tell you for certain that I am the gate for the sheep. **8** Everyone who came before me was a thief or a robber, and the sheep did not listen to any of them. **9** I am the gate. All who come in through me will be saved. Through me they will come and go and find pasture. **10** A thief comes only to rob, kill, and destroy. I came so that everyone would have life, and have it fully. **11** I am the good shepherd, and the good shepherd gives up his life for his sheep. **12** Hired workers are not like the shepherd. They don't own the sheep, and when they see a wolf coming, they run off and leave the sheep. Then the wolf attacks and scatters the flock. **13** Hired workers run away because they don't care about the sheep. **14** I am the good shepherd. I know my sheep, and they know me. **15** Just as the Father knows me, I know the Father, and I give up my life for my sheep.

In John's gospel Jesus also says he is bread, light, the vine, the resurrection, the way, the truth and the life.

Q What was Jesus willing to give up? What did this mean for him?

Q What would you look for in a good leader?

R84 **Famous last words**

Jesus and his disciples are in Jerusalem. Jesus knows he only has a few more hours with his closest friends before being arrested. He prepares his friends by telling them about how they can live after he has gone.

JOHN 14:1–7,15–17

1 Jesus said to his disciples, "Don't be worried! Have faith in God and have faith in me. **2** There are many rooms in my **Father's** house. I wouldn't tell you this, unless it was true. I am going there to prepare a place for each of you. **3** After I have done this, I will come back and take you with me. Then we will be together. **4** You know the way to where I am going."

5 Thomas said, "Lord, we don't even know where you are going! How can we know the way?"

6 "I am the way, the truth, and the life!" Jesus answered. "Without me, no one can go to the Father. **7** If you had known me, you would have known the Father. But from now on, you do know him, and you have seen him…"

15 Jesus said to his disciples:

> If you love me, you will do as I command. **16** Then I will ask the Father to send you the **Holy Spirit** who will help you and always be with you. **17** The Spirit will show you what is true. The people of this world cannot accept the Spirit, because they don't see or know him. But you know the Spirit, who is with you and will keep on living in you.

Q Who will help the disciples in the same way that Jesus had done?

Q If you had to leave your friends, what would you want to say to them?

I don't know him!

When Peter hears that Jesus is going away, he says that he would follow Jesus anywhere – even die for him. Jesus warns that Peter will say he doesn't know Jesus – not once, but three times before the cock crows at the start of the next day. Jesus is arrested (R58) and taken to the high priest's house. John follows with Peter.

JOHN 18:15–18,25–27

15 Simon Peter and another disciple followed Jesus. That disciple knew the **high priest**, and he followed Jesus into the courtyard of the high priest's house. **16** Peter stayed outside near the gate. But the other disciple came back out and spoke to the girl at the gate. She let Peter go in, **17** but asked him, "Aren't you one of that man's followers?"

"No, I am not!" Peter answered.

18 It was cold, and the servants and temple police had made a charcoal fire. They were warming themselves around it, when Peter went over and stood near the fire to warm himself…

> **Verse 15** In John's gospel, 'another disciple', or 'favourite disciple' is John himself.
>
> **Verse 27** Cockerels crow at the start of a new day. This was the start of Friday, the day on which Jesus died.

25 While Simon Peter was standing there warming himself, someone asked him, "Aren't you one of Jesus' followers?"

Again Peter denied it and said, "No, I am not!"

26 One of the high priest's servants was there. He was a relative of the servant whose ear Peter had cut off, and he asked, "Didn't I see you in the garden with that man?"

27 Once more Peter denied it, and at once a cock crowed.

Q Peter has been one of Jesus' closest friends. Why does he pretend he doesn't know Jesus?

Q When you feel scared, how does it change the way that you behave?

Everything is done

Jesus' mother, Mary, has been among the crowd following Jesus. She has seen him heal, teach and lead – and now she is watching him die.

JOHN 19:25-30

25 Jesus' mother stood beside his cross with her sister and Mary the wife of Clopas. Mary Magdalene was standing there too. **26** When Jesus saw his mother and his favourite disciple with her, he said to his mother, "This man is now your son." **27** Then he said to the disciple, "She is now your mother." From then on, that disciple took her into his own home. **28** Jesus knew that he had now finished his work. And in order to make the **Scriptures** come true, he said, "I am thirsty!" **29** A jar of cheap wine was there. Someone then soaked a sponge with the wine and held it up to Jesus' mouth on the stem of a hyssop plant. **30** After Jesus drank the wine, he said, "Everything is done!" He bowed his head and died.

Mary – IP6, page 100 R67, R68

Jesus' words from the cross R60, R79

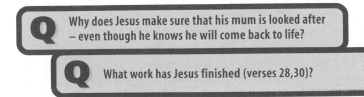

Q Why does Jesus make sure that his mum is looked after – even though he knows he will come back to life?

Q What work has Jesus finished (verses 28,30)?

Jesus and Peter

John and Mary have watched Jesus die, and Nicodemus helps to bury him. Two days later, when Mary goes to the place where he was buried, Jesus isn't there! He has come back to life.

Simon Peter, one of Jesus' closest friends, has let Jesus down. Simon suggests that the disciples go fishing. Jesus appears and helps them to catch a huge number of fish. But what will Jesus say to Simon Peter?

Nicodemus
R81

Back to
life
R61

Peter
R85

JOHN 21:15–22

15 When Jesus and his disciples had finished eating, he asked, "Simon son of John, do you love me more than the others do?"

Simon Peter answered, "Yes, Lord, you know I do!"

"Then feed my lambs," Jesus said.

16 Jesus asked a second time, "Simon son of John, do you love me?"

Peter answered, "Yes, Lord, you know I love you!"

"Then take care of my sheep," Jesus told him.

17 Jesus asked a third time, "Simon son of John, do you love me?"

Peter was hurt because Jesus had asked him three times if he loved him. So he told Jesus, "Lord, you know everything. You know I love you."

Jesus replied, "Feed my sheep. **18** I tell you for certain that when you were a young man, you dressed yourself and went wherever you wanted to go. But when you are old, you will hold out your hands. Then others will tie your belt around you and lead you where you don't want to go."

19 Jesus said this to tell how Peter would die and bring honour to God. Then he said to Peter, "Follow me!"

20 Peter turned and saw Jesus' favourite disciple following them. He was the same one who had sat next to Jesus at the meal and had asked, "Lord, who is going to betray you?"

21 When Peter saw that disciple, he asked Jesus, "Lord, what about him?"

22 Jesus answered, "What is it to you, if I want him to live until I return? You must follow me."

> **Q** Why does Jesus ask the same question three times?

Going up

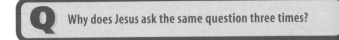

Luke's first book in the *New Testament,* Luke's gospel (R67–79) was about Jesus and what he did. His second book is about Jesus' followers and what they did. It's called The Acts of the Apostles. An apostle is someone who is sent on a mission – and the mission is about to begin...

ACTS 1:1–11

1 Theophilus, I first wrote to you about all that Jesus did and taught from the very first **2** until he was taken up to **heaven**. But before he was taken up, he gave orders to the **apostles** he had chosen with the help of the **Holy Spirit**.

3 For forty days after Jesus had suffered and died, he proved in many ways that he had been raised from death. He appeared to his apostles and spoke to them about **God's kingdom**. **4** While he was still with them, he said:

Don't leave Jerusalem yet. Wait here for the Father to give you the Holy Spirit, just as I told you he has promised to do. **5** John **baptized** with water, but in a few days you will be baptized with the Holy Spirit.

6 While the apostles were still with Jesus, they asked him,

Mary – IP6, page 100, R67, R68

> **Verse 1** Theophilus is Luke's friend. His name also means 'someone who loves God'.
> **Verse 8** **Jerusalem** was the capital city, Judea the disciples' home country and Samaria was the next country.

"Lord, are you now going to give Israel its own king again?"

7 Jesus said to them, "You don't need to know the time of those events that only the Father controls. **8** But the Holy Spirit will come upon you and give you power. Then you will tell everyone about me in Jerusalem, in all Judea, in Samaria, and everywhere in the world."

9 After Jesus had said this and

The Ascension: Jesus left his friends and they didn't see him any more. It isn't exactly clear how this happened. The Bible says that Jesus 'was taken up', so Christians call it Jesus' 'Ascension', which means going up.

while they were watching, he was taken up into a cloud. They could not see him, **10** but as he went up, they kept looking up into the sky.

Suddenly two men dressed in white clothes were standing there beside them. **11** They said, "Why are you men from Galilee standing here and looking up into the sky? Jesus has been taken to heaven. But he will come back in the same way that you have seen him go."

Q What was the mission that the apostles had to carry out?

R89

Acts 2:1–13

Speaking out

After Jesus leaves his *disciples*, they stay in *Jerusalem*. Ten days later, Jewish believers from many countries come to Jerusalem to celebrate Pentecost, a harvest festival. Jesus has promised his followers that they will be baptised with the *Holy Spirit*.

ACTS 2:1–13

1 On the day of **Pentecost** all the Lord's followers were together in one place. **2** Suddenly there was a noise from heaven like the sound of a mighty wind! It filled the house where they were meeting. **3** Then they saw what looked like fiery tongues moving in all directions, and a tongue came and settled on each person there. **4** The **Holy Spirit** took control of everyone, and they began speaking whatever languages the Spirit let them speak.

5 Many religious Jews from every country in the world were living in Jerusalem. **6** And when they heard this noise, a crowd gathered. But they were surprised, because they were hearing everything in their own languages. **7** They were excited and amazed, and said:

Don't all these who are speaking come from Galilee? **8** Then why do we hear them speaking our very own languages? **9** Some of us are from Parthia, Media, and Elam. Others are from

> **Verse 9-11** These countries are all around Judea – north, south, east and west.

Mesopotamia, Judea, Cappadocia, Pontus, Asia, **10** Phrygia, Pamphylia, Egypt, parts of Libya near Cyrene, Rome, **11** Crete, and Arabia. Some of us were born Jews, and others of us have chosen to be Jews. Yet we all hear them using our own languages to tell the wonderful things God has done.

12 Everyone was excited and confused. Some of them even kept asking each other, "What does all this mean?"

13 Others made fun of the Lord's followers and said, "They are drunk."

The story continues...

Peter, filled with power from God's Holy Spirit, tells the crowd that one of God's promises is coming true – God will give his Spirit to everyone. God has kept another promise – he sent them a Messiah to rescue them – Jesus. Three thousand people believe Peter's message.

> **Q** The Holy Spirit can't be seen – but what did the followers see and hear?

> **Q** Think of a time when you believed something was true after hearing someone tell you.

Get up!

After the Holy Spirit comes to Jesus' followers, Peter and John become their leaders.

ACTS 3:1–10; 4:1–4

1 The time of prayer was about three o'clock in the afternoon, and Peter and John were going into the **temple**. **2** A man who had been born lame was being carried to the temple door. Each day he was placed beside this door, known as the Beautiful Gate. He sat there and begged from the people who were going in.

3 The man saw Peter and John entering the temple, and he asked them for money. **4** But they looked straight at him and said, "Look up at us!"

5 The man stared at them and thought he was going to get something. **6** But Peter said, "I don't have any silver or gold! But I will give you what I do have. In the name of Jesus Christ from Nazareth, get up and start walking." **7** Peter then took him by the right hand and helped him up.

At once the man's feet and ankles became strong, **8** and he jumped up and started walking. He went with Peter and John into the temple, walking and jumping and praising God. **9** Everyone saw him walking around and praising God. **10** They knew that he was the beggar who had been lying beside the Beautiful Gate, and they were completely surprised. They could not imagine what had happened to the man.

ACTS 4:1–4

1 The apostles were still talking to the people, when some **priests**, the captain of the temple guard, and some **Sadducees** arrived. **2** These men were angry because the **apostles** were teaching the people that the dead would be raised from death, just as Jesus had been raised from death. **3** It was already late in the afternoon, and they arrested Peter and John and put them in jail for the night. **4** But a lot of people who had heard the message believed it. So by now there were about five thousand followers of the Lord.

The story continues…

The same leaders who had arrested Jesus now bring Peter and John to trial. Peter speaks again with the power of the Holy Spirit, and the leaders have to let them go. The group of followers continues to grow. They pray together and share everything with each other.

R61

Q What was the man at the temple door hoping to get? What did he receive?

Q Think of a time when you believed something was true after seeing it yourself.

R91

Acts 9:1-9, 17-19

Stop!

The priests and leaders are worried. They had seen Jesus put to death – now his followers are preaching the same message that Jesus had preached. They arrest and kill a follower called Stephen. A young man called Saul watches Stephen die and decides that he will also stop these followers talking about Jesus.

IP9

ACTS 9:1–9

1 Saul kept on threatening to kill the **Lord's** followers. He even went to the high **priest 2** and asked for letters to the Jewish leaders in Damascus. He did this because he wanted to arrest and take to **Jerusalem** any man or woman who had accepted **the Lord's Way. 3** When Saul had almost reached Damascus, a bright light from **heaven** suddenly flashed around him. **4** He fell to the ground and heard a voice that said, "Saul! Saul! Why are you so cruel to me?"

5 "Who are you?" Saul asked.

"I am Jesus," the Lord answered. "I am the one you are so cruel to. **6** Now get up and go into the city, where you will be told what to do."

7 The men with Saul stood there speechless. They had heard the voice, but they had not seen anyone. **8** Saul got up from the ground, and when he opened his eyes, he could not see a thing. Someone then led him by the hand to Damascus, **9** and for three days he was blind and did not eat or drink.

The story continues...

God tells Ananias, a follower in Damascus, to visit Saul and pray for him – Saul has been chosen to tell non-Jews about Jesus. Ananias is terrified but obeys.

ACTS 9:17–19

17 Ananias left and went into the house where Saul was staying. Ananias placed his hands on him and said, "Saul, the Lord Jesus has sent me. He is the same one who appeared to you along the road. He wants you to be able to see and to be filled with the Holy Spirit."

18 Suddenly something like fish scales fell from Saul's eyes, and he could see. He got up and was baptized. **19** Then he ate and felt much better.

For several days Saul stayed with the Lord's followers in Damascus.

Q What changed Saul from being an enemy of Jesus' followers to becoming a follower himself?

Q How will the other believers feel about having Saul in their group?

Paul

Also known as Saul

⭐ Star factor

★ Would do anything to
tell people about Jesus

Key Bible verse

"I have chosen him to tell foreigners, kings and
the people of Israel about me." *Acts 9:15*

Big events in Paul's life

Brightest	Saw a light on the road to Damascus which led to… (R91)
Darkest	Was blinded for three days (R91)
Most life-changing	Heard Jesus on the road and followed him forever (R91)
Loudest	Sang hymns at midnight in prison with his friend Silas, in an earthquake (R93)
Wettest	Was shipwrecked and saved the lives of everyone on board (R94)
Longest	People read his words over 2000 years after he wrote them

Mary

Jesus

1st Century

1st Century

C
E

What the Bible says about Paul

★ He knew the Scriptures well and studied with the best Jewish teachers

★ He was a Roman citizen

★ He had a job making tents and worked as a tent maker for over a year in Corinth while telling people about Jesus

★ A dramatic event (and a scared Christian) turned Paul's life round (R91)

★ About half of the New Testament is made up of Paul's writing (R96–99)

★ He was often in prison but used these times to write letters or speak to other prisoners

More about Paul

Escaped in a basket
Acts 9:23–25

Revives a young man who fell asleep and fell out of a window
Acts 20:9–12

In Paul's lifetime

Roman roads and great buildings like the Colosseum were being built.

Sailing boats were the main form of travel around the Mediterranean.

Roman rulers try to stop people becoming Christians.

Peter

Paul

1st Century

1st Century

Drama in Philippi

Three years later, Paul (who has changed his name from Saul) starts taking the message about Jesus to other countries. He travels with helpers like Barnabas, Mark (who probably wrote Mark's gospel) Timothy, Silas and Luke the doctor, who writes about the journeys. They have just arrived in Greece.

ACTS 16:12–18

12 From there we went to Philippi, which is a Roman colony in the first district of Macedonia.

We spent several days in Philippi. **13** Then on the **Sabbath** we went outside the city gate to a place by the river, where we thought there would be a Jewish meeting place for prayer. We sat down and talked with the women who came. **14** One of them was Lydia, who was from the city of Thyatira and sold

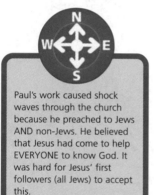

Paul's work caused shock waves through the church because he preached to Jews AND non-Jews. He believed that Jesus had come to help EVERYONE to know God. It was hard for Jesus' first followers (all Jews) to accept this.

expensive purple cloth. She was a worshipper of the Lord God, and he made her willing to accept what Paul was saying. **15** Then after she and her family were **baptized**, she kept on begging us, "If you think I really do have faith in the Lord, come and stay in my home." Finally, we accepted her invitation.

16 One day on our way to the place of prayer, we were met by a slave girl. She had a spirit in her that gave her the power to tell the future. By doing this she made a lot of money for her owners. **17** The girl followed Paul and the rest of us and kept yelling, "These men are servants of the Most High God! They are telling you how to be saved."

18 This went on for several days. Finally, Paul got so upset that he turned and said to the spirit, "In the name of Jesus Christ, I order you to leave this girl alone!" At once the evil spirit left her.

> **Q** What sort of a person does Paul seem to be in these two stories (R92,R93)?

Earthquake!  R93

The story continues...

ACTS 16:19–34

19 When the girl's owners realized that they had lost all chances for making more money, they grabbed Paul and Silas and dragged them into court. **20** They told the officials, "These Jews are upsetting our city! **21** They are telling us to do things we Romans are not allowed to do."

22 The crowd joined in the attack on Paul and Silas. Then the officials tore the clothes off the two men and ordered them to be beaten with a whip. **23** After they had been badly beaten, they were put in jail, and the jailer was told to guard them carefully. **24** The jailer did as he was told. He put them deep inside the jail and chained their feet to heavy blocks of wood.

25 About midnight Paul and Silas were praying and singing praises to God, while the other prisoners listened.

26 Suddenly a strong earthquake shook the jail to its foundations. The doors opened, and the chains fell from all the prisoners.

27 When the jailer woke up and saw that the doors were open, he thought that the prisoners had escaped. He pulled out his sword and was about to kill himself. **28** But Paul shouted, "Don't harm yourself! No one has escaped."

29 The jailer asked for a torch and went into the jail. He was shaking all over as he knelt down in front of Paul and Silas. **30** After he had led them out of the jail, he asked, "What must I do to be saved?"

> **Verse 29** The jailer's torch would have had a wooden handle. At the top were rags soaked in oil which he set alight.

31 They replied, "Have faith in the Lord Jesus and you will be saved! This is also true for everyone who lives in your home."

32 Then Paul and Silas told him and everyone else in his house about the Lord. **33** While it was still night, the jailer took them to a place where he could wash their cuts and bruises. Then he and everyone in his home were **baptized**. **34** They were very glad that they had put their faith in God. After this, the jailer took Paul and Silas to his home and gave them something to eat.

Q Who would you most like to be in this story?

Q Why does speaking about Jesus cause trouble for Paul and Silas? (R92 and 93)

Shipwreck!

Paul continues to travel around the eastern Mediterranean, telling people about Jesus. Eventually he is arrested and held prisoner in Jerusalem for two years. He appeals to the Roman Emperor, so he has to go to Rome under the guard of Captain Julius. But their ship gets caught in a terrible storm. It is late September – the weather in the Mediterranean Sea would not be good for sailing.

ACTS 27:20–39,43–44;28:1–2

20 For several days we could not see either the sun or the stars. A strong wind kept blowing, and we finally gave up all hope of being saved.

21 Since none of us had eaten anything for a long time, Paul stood up and told the men:

> You should have listened to me! If you had stayed on in Crete, you would not have had this damage and loss. **22** But now I beg you to cheer up, because you will be safe. Only the ship will be lost. **23** I belong to God, and I worship him. Last night he sent an **angel 24** to tell me, "Paul, don't be afraid! You will stand trial before the Emperor. And because of you, God will save the lives of everyone on the ship." **25** Cheer up! I am sure that God will do exactly what he promised. **26** But we will first be shipwrecked on some island.

27 For fourteen days and nights we had been blown around over the Mediterranean Sea. But about midnight the sailors realized that we were getting near land. **28** They measured and found that the water was about forty metres deep. A little later they measured again and found it was only about thirty metres. **29** The sailors were afraid that we might hit some rocks, and they let down four anchors from the back of the ship. Then they prayed for daylight.

30 The sailors wanted to escape from the ship. So they lowered the lifeboat into the water, pretending that they were letting down an anchor from the front of the ship. **31** But Paul said to Captain Julius and the soldiers, "If the sailors don't stay on the ship, you won't have any chance to save your lives." **32** The soldiers then cut the ropes that held the lifeboat and let it fall into the sea.

33 Just before daylight Paul begged the people to eat something. He told them, "For fourteen days you have been so worried that you haven't eaten a thing. **34** I beg you to eat something. Your lives depend on it. Do this and not one of you will be hurt."

35 After Paul had said this, he took a piece of bread and gave thanks to God. Then in front of everyone, he broke the bread and ate some. **36** They all felt encouraged, and each of them ate something. **37** There were 276 people on the ship, **38** and after everyone had eaten, they threw the cargo of wheat into the sea to make the ship lighter.

39 Morning came, and the ship's crew saw a coast that they did not recognize. But they did see a cove with a beach. So they decided to try to run the ship aground on the beach…

43 Captain Julius … ordered everyone who could swim to dive into the water and head for shore. **44** Then he told the others to hold on to planks of wood or parts of the ship. At last, everyone safely reached shore.

ACTS 28:1–2

1 When we came ashore, we learnt that the island was called Malta. **2** The local people were very friendly, and they welcomed us by building a fire, because it was rainy and cold.

The story continues…

Paul arrives safely in Rome. He can't leave his house as a soldier is there to guard him, but for two years, visitors come and Paul tells them about Jesus. Luke ends his book here, and does not write what happened to Paul after this.

Q How do you think Luke (the writer) felt during the storm? What was the worst point for him? Why does he describe it in such detail?

Q Where else in *Into the Bible* can you find someone who takes bread and gives thanks to God?

No barriers

Before travelling to Rome, Paul writes a letter to the Christians there. He wants them to understand how much God loves them.

31 If God is on our side, can anyone be against us? **32** God did not keep back his own Son, but he gave him for us. If God did this, won't he freely give us everything else? **33** If God says his chosen ones are acceptable to him, can anyone bring charges against them? **34** Or can anyone condemn them? No indeed! **Christ** died and was raised to life, and now he is at God's right side, speaking to him for us.

35 Can anything separate us from the love of Christ? Can trouble, suffering, and hard times, or hunger and nakedness, or danger and death? **36** It is exactly as the Scriptures say,

> "For you we face death all day long. We are like sheep on their way to be butchered."

37 In everything we have won more than a victory because of Christ who loves us. **38** I am sure that nothing

Letters and numbers
Thirteen of Paul's letters are in the Bible, named by the person or place who received the letter. If Paul wrote more than one letter to the same place or person, these letters have numbers – 1 Corinthians, 2 Timothy. Letters by Peter and John are also in the New Testament.

can separate us from God's love—not life or death, not angels or spirits, not the present or the future, **39** and not powers above or powers below. Nothing in all creation can separate us from God's love for us in Christ Jesus our Lord!

> **Q** Why would you say Paul continues to believe in God even in trouble, suffering and hard times?

R56

Paul – IP9, page 166

R96

Eat, drink and remember

Christians, like those at the church in Corinth in Greece, remembered God's rescue plan with a meal of bread and wine. They called it the Lord's Supper. Paul writes them a letter to help them understand about being Christians, and explains the Lord's Supper.

1 CORINTHIANS 11:23–26

23 I have already told you what the Lord Jesus did on the night he was betrayed. And it came from the Lord himself.

He took some bread in his hands. **24** Then after he had given thanks, he broke it and said, "This is my body, which is given for you. Eat this and remember me."

25 After the meal, Jesus took a cup of wine in his hands and said, "This is my blood, and with it God makes his new agreement with you. Drink this and remember me."

26 The Lord meant that when you eat this bread and drink from this cup, you tell about his death until he comes.

Christians all over the world still use these words when they remember Jesus' death. They may call this the Lord's Supper, Holy Communion, Eucharist or breaking of bread.

Q Paul wasn't there when Jesus said these words. How do you think he knew what Jesus had said?

Q What do you do to remember something (or someone) special?

Love

Paul also tells the Corinthians that the *Holy Spirit* gives them gifts or abilities to use for God. Paul writes: "I want you to desire the best gifts. So I will show you a much better way." This 'better way' has become a favourite part of the Bible for many people:

1 CORINTHIANS 13:1–13
1 What if I could speak all languages of humans and of **angels**? If I did not love others, I would be nothing more than a noisy gong or a clanging cymbal.

2 What if I could **prophesy** and understand all secrets and all knowledge? And what if I had faith that moved mountains? I would be nothing, unless I loved others.

This part of the Bible is sometimes read at weddings. Why do you think this is?

3 What if I gave away all that I owned and let myself be burnt alive? I would gain nothing, unless I loved others.

4 Love is kind and patient, never jealous, boastful, proud, or **5** rude.

Love isn't selfish or quick-tempered.

It doesn't keep a record of wrongs that others do.

6 Love rejoices in the truth, but not in evil.

7 Love is always supportive, loyal, hopeful, and trusting.

8 Love never fails! Everyone who **prophesies** will stop, and **unknown languages** will no longer be spoken. All that we know will be forgotten.

9 We don't know everything, and our prophecies are not complete.

10 But what is perfect will some day appear, and what isn't perfect will then disappear.

11 When we were children, we thought and reasoned as children do. But when we grew up, we stopped our childish ways.

12 Now all we can see of God is like a cloudy picture in a mirror. Later we will see him face to face. We don't know everything, but then we will, just as God completely understands us.

13 For now there are faith, hope, and love. But of these three, the greatest is love.

 How would you answer the question, "What is love?"?

 Can you make up a poem about faith, hope or love?

How to live

Paul's time in Philippi was full of adventures, and he always remembered the new believers that he met there. Later he wrote to the new church at Philippi. The rich woman, the slave girl and the jailer could have been with the other believers when these words were first read out...

R92

PHILIPPIANS 2:1–13

1 Christ encourages you, and his love comforts you. God's **Spirit** unites you, and you are concerned for others. **2** Now make me completely happy! Live in harmony by showing love for each other. Be united in what you think, as if you were only one person. **3** Don't be jealous or proud, but be humble and consider others more important than yourselves. **4** Care about them as much as you care about

The church When people started to believe the message about Jesus, they met other believers. These groups were known as the church – people who were 'called out'. At first they met in houses. They did not have a special building.

yourselves **5** and think the same way that Christ Jesus thought:

> **6** Christ was truly God. But he did not try to remain equal with God.
>
> **7** Instead he gave up everything and became a slave, when he became like one of us.
>
> **8** Christ was humble. He obeyed God and even died on a cross.
>
> **9** Then God gave Christ the highest place and honoured his name above all others.
>
> **10** So at the name of Jesus everyone will bow down, those in **heaven**, on earth, and under the earth.
>
> **11** And to the glory of God the **Father** everyone will openly agree, "Jesus Christ is Lord!"

12 My dear friends, you always obeyed when I was with you. Now that I am away, you should obey even more. So work with fear and trembling to discover what it really means to be saved. **13** God is working in you to make you willing and able to obey him.

> **Q** What would a Philippian believer learn about Jesus from reading (or hearing) this part of Paul's letter?

God's Word

One of Paul's friends is a young man called Timothy. Timothy has travelled with Paul and is now the leader of the Christians at Ephesus (in Turkey). Paul writes two letters to Timothy, to encourage him in his faith and his work.

2 TIMOTHY 3:14–17
14 Keep on being faithful to what you were taught and to

what you believed. After all, you know who taught you these things.

15 Since childhood, you have known the Holy **Scriptures** that are able to make you wise enough to have faith in **Christ** Jesus and be saved. **16** Everything in the Scriptures is God's Word. All of it is useful for teaching and helping people

Verse 15 The Scriptures that Timothy and Paul knew were the Old Testament – God's message to the Jewish people.

and for correcting them and showing them how to live.

17 The Scriptures train God's servants to do all kinds of good deeds

Christians believe that the Old and New Testaments are God's word to them – the Bible guides them in how they live and what they believe. When they hear or read the Bible, it's as if God is speaking to them directly.

Q How does the Bible affect what people believe? How does it affect how people act?

R100 **Heaven**

John has been sent to the island of Patmos as a punishment for believing in Jesus. One Sunday when he is worshipping God, he has a vision. He sees amazing pictures of Jesus, heaven and the future. He writes this down to share with all believers.

The writer of Revelation is called John. It could be John the disciple, who knew Jesus well.

The style of writing in Revelation is called apocalyptic, which means that it is about things that happen at the end of time.

REVELATION 4:1–6

1 After this, I looked and saw a door that opened into **heaven**. Then the voice that had spoken to me at first and that sounded like a trumpet said, "Come up here! I will show you what must happen next." **2** At once the **Spirit** took control of me, and there in heaven I saw a throne and someone sitting on it. **3** The one who was sitting there sparkled like precious stones of jasper and carnelian. A rainbow that looked like an emerald surrounded the throne.

Verse 3 These are all precious stones or jewels – jasper is opaque, reddish-brown, carnelian is red, emerald is green.

4 Twenty-four other thrones were in a circle around that throne. And on each of these thrones there was an elder dressed in white clothes and wearing a gold crown. **5** Flashes of lightning and roars of thunder came out from the throne in the centre of the circle. Seven torches, which are the seven spirits of God, were burning in front of the throne. **6** Also in front of the throne was something that looked like a glass sea, clear as crystal.

Around the throne in the centre were four living creatures covered front and back with eyes.

> **Q** How would you describe the place where God is? Write or draw your 'picture'.

The end

John describes many awesome events that he sees in heaven and on earth. He ends by going back to the beginning. John's 'pictures' would remind readers of the creation of the world and the separation of God and people and would give them hope for a different future.

REVELATION 21:1–6

1 I saw a new **heaven** and a new earth. The first heaven and the first earth had disappeared, and so had the sea. **2** Then I saw New **Jerusalem**, that holy city, coming down from God in heaven. It was like a bride dressed in her wedding gown and ready to meet her husband.

R1, R2

3 I heard a loud voice shout from the throne:

God's home is now with his people. He will live with them, and they will be his own. Yes, God will make his home among his people. **4** He will wipe all tears from their eyes, and there will be no more death, suffering, crying, or pain. These things of the past are gone for ever.

5 Then the one sitting on the throne said:

I am making everything new. Write down what I have said. My words are true and can be trusted. **6** Everything is finished! I am Alpha and Omega, the beginning and the end. I will freely give water from the life-giving fountain to everyone who is thirsty.

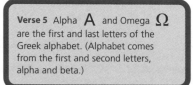

Verse 5 Alpha A and Omega Ω are the first and last letters of the Greek alphabet. (Alphabet comes from the first and second letters, alpha and beta.)

REVELATION 22:1–5

1 The angel showed me a river that was crystal clear, and its waters gave life. The river came from the throne where God and the Lamb were seated. **2** Then it flowed down the middle of the city's main street. On each side of the river are trees that grow a different kind of fruit each month of the year. The fruit gives life, and the leaves are used as medicine to heal the nations.

Verse 22:1
Lamb:The Lamb is a word picture for Jesus.

3 God's **curse** will no longer be on the people of that city. He and the Lamb will be seated there on their thrones, and its people will worship God **4** and will see him face to face. God's name will be written on the foreheads of the people. **5** Never again will night appear, and no one who lives there will ever need a lamp or the sun. The Lord God will be their light, and they will rule for ever.

Q How do you feel when you read about the future?

Q How do John's words give hope for the future? What are your hopes for the future?

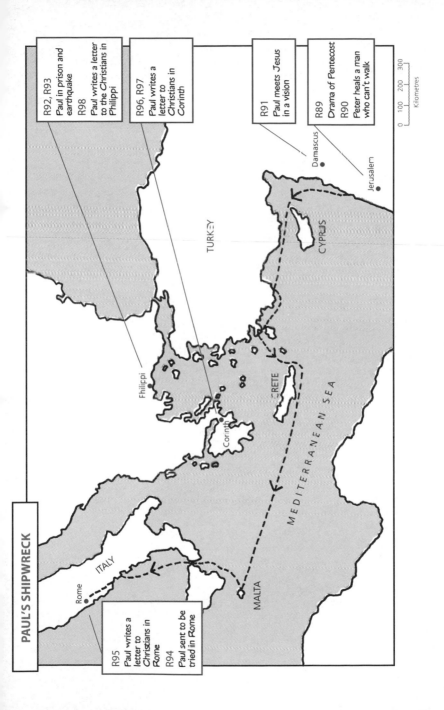

PAUL'S SHIPWRECK

R92, R93
Paul in prison and earthquake

R98
Paul writes a letter to the Christians in Philippi

R96, R97
Paul writes a letter to Christians in Corinth

R91
Paul meets Jesus in a vision

R89
Drama of Pentecost

R90
Peter heals a man who can't walk

R95
Paul writes a letter to Christians in Rome

R94
Paul sent to be tried in Rome

TURKEY

Damascus

Jerusalem

CYPRUS

Philippi

Corinth

CRETE

MEDITERRANEAN SEA

ITALY

Rome

MALTA

0   100   200   300
Kilometres

Glossary

(All words in **bold** are to be found in this glossary)

altar	a special place to worship God, originally made of stones – later became a kind of table in the **temple**
ancestor	going back a long way in time, someone that you are descended from, eg a great-great-great-grandparent. That makes you a descendant.
angel	a messenger from God
apostle	someone who is sent out; one of the disciples of Jesus after he had returned to heaven
Babylon	capital of Babylonian empire, in the area of Iraq
baptise/baptize	to dip a person in water, as a sign that they believe in God
bless/blessing	God giving something special; calling for good things to happen to someone else
Book of the Law	See 'Law'
Christ	the Greek word for **Messiah**. Often used as part of the name Jesus Christ (or Christ Jesus).
commandments	laws or rules to help people live in God's way
covenant	agreement or treaty between two sides
curse	the opposite of blessing; calling for bad things to happen to someone else
descendants	your children, grandchildren, great-grandchildren – everyone who will be born in the future in one family
disciple	a student or learner. anyone who followed a **teacher.** The 12 disciples were the closest followers of Jesus.
eternal	going on for ever; without end
eternal life	living for ever with God

exile	to be sent out of your country as a punishment
Father	when spoken by Jesus, or written in the New Testament letters, Father with a capital letter refers to God
Galilee	the area where Jesus lived, about 100km from Jerusalem – see map page 121
Gethsemane	means 'olive press'; a garden just outside Jerusalem
gospel	translation of the Greek word for 'good news'; one of the four books about Jesus in the New Testament
Great Day of Forgiveness	Day of Atonement, Yom Kippur – a day when Jewish people say sorry to God for the wrong things they have done
Greek	a person from Greece; the language spoke by people from Greece
heaven	a place where God is, a place of rest
Hebrew	see **Israelite**; also the language spoken by the Israelites
high priest	the leader of all the priests
holy	separated, set apart or special to God
Holy Spirit	God in a form that can't be seen; the invisible presence of God (see R50)
idol	something that is worshipped instead of God, could be represented by a statue
Israel	the Northern kingdom (the country divided after King Solomon died)
Israelite	people who were descended from Jacob, also known as Israel. (They were known as 'the people of Israel' long before there was a country called Israel.)
Jew/Jewish	name originally given to people descended from Judah, one of Jacob's sons
Jerusalem	capital city of Judah, site of the temple
Judah	the Southern kingdom (the country divided after King Solomon died)
Judea	where many Jews lived in Roman times – see map page 121

kingdom of God, kingdom of heaven	living in the way that God wants; God's rule
Latin	the language of the Roman empire
Law (Law of Moses)	the first five books of the Old Testament
LORD (in capitals)	stands for a very special name that describes who God is. Jewish people would never say this word – instead they said Adonai, which is translated as 'LORD'.
Lord	the disciples sometimes called Jesus 'Lord', but it was the word 'Adon' which meant 'Master' or 'Sir'.
Messiah	the chosen or anointed person who God would use to save his people
miracle	in the Bible, an act or event that could only be brought about by God
New Testament	the second part of the Bible, mainly about Jesus
offerings	gifts of food or money brought to God
Old Testament	the first part of the Bible
olive oil	oil made from crushing and pressing olives; pouring olive oil over someone's head (anointing) showed they were 'set apart' for God as a king or priest
paradise	see heaven
Passover	a Jewish feast commemorating the escape of the Jewish people from Egypt
Pentecost	the first harvest festival celebrated by Jewish people; Christians now celebrate Pentecost as the time when the Holy Spirit came
Pharisees	Jewish men who followed strict rules to try to please God. Jesus disagreed with Pharisees who loved rules more than they loved God.
pilgrimage	journey made as part of a person's faith
priest	a man chosen by God to to lead worship and offer sacrifices

prophecy/prophecies	(noun) a message spoken by a prophet about something happening now or in the future
prophesy	(verb) to speak a prophetic message
prophets	men and women who tell messages from God
psalm	a song to, or about, God
Sabbath	Saturday, the seventh day – a day of rest for Jews
sacred	holy, something special to God
sacred chest	also known as the ark of the covenant: a box, covered in gold, decorated with two golden angels and carried on poles. The ten commandments were inside it. For the Jewish people, it was a sign that God was with them.
sacrifice	comes from the same word as sacred. Something that you give up, an offering. In the Old Testament times, this involved killing an animal such as a cow or a sheep.
Sadducees	members of a strict Jewish religious group
Samaria	the area between Galilee and Judea; people who lived there were Samaritans, Samaritans and Jews were enemies.
Satan/devil	an angel who became God's enemy
Saviour	someone who saves another person; word used for Jesus, meaning that he rescued people from **sin**
Scriptures	something that is written down; The Bible uses it to refer to the Old Testament
sin	choosing not to live as God wants
sinner	a person whose lifestyle means they weren't following God
sling	a weapon for throwing stones
Son of David	a name for the Messiah – used about Jesus
Son of Man	a name that Jesus uses for himself
Spirit of the Lord/God	see Holy Spirit
tax collector	a Jewish person who collected taxes for the Romans

teacher	translates the Jewish word Rabbi, someone who could teach others about God's truth
temple	the building in Jerusalem where Jews went to worship God
testament	a legal agreement
tomb	a cave where dead people were buried. To stop animals or robbers taking the body, the opening was closed with a large round stone.
unclean	a food or animal which meant that a Jew couldn't be holy
unknown languages	one of the gifts that the Holy Spirit gives is to enable people to speak in a different language
worship	an act that puts God first, often singing or praying
Zion	one of the hills in Jerusalem

Names

Abram/Abraham	the ancestor of all Jewish people
Adam	the first man
Ahab	a bad king of Israel
Andrew	brother of Peter, one of Jesus' 12 disciples
Benjamin	Jacob's youngest son
David	a great king of Judah and Israel; shepherd, soldier and singer
Elijah	an Old Testament **prophet**
Esau	one of Isaac's twin sons
Eve	the first woman
Hagar	Sarai's Egyptian slave girl, who has Abram's child
Isaac	son of Abraham and Sarah; father of Esau and Jacob
Isaiah	an Old Testament **prophet**
Ishmael	son of Abram and Hagar
Israel	see Jacob
Jacob	one of Isaac's twin sons; God re-named him Israel

Jeremiah	an Old Testament **prophet**
John	one of Jesus' 12 disciples, wrote about Jesus (R80)
John the Baptist	cousin of Jesus, spoke to crowds to prepare the way for Jesus
Joseph (NT)	the husband of Mary
Joseph (OT)	Jacob's favourite son; a ruler in Egypt
Josiah	a young king of Judah who obeyed God
Judah	one of Jacob's 12 sons
King David	see David
Luke	a doctor, wrote two books about Jesus and his followers
Mark	a young man who knew Jesus and wrote about him
Mary	Jewish woman who became the mother of Jesus
Mary (Magdalene)	a friend of Jesus
Matthew	one of Jesus' 12 disciples, wrote about Jesus
Nathan	a prophet who told King David the truth
Noah	obeyed God by building a boat to save his family and animals from a worldwide flood
Paul/Saul	a Jew who changed from hating followers of Jesus to becoming a bold speaker about Jesus; travelled all round the Mediterranean area and wrote many letters (some in the New Testament)
Peter/Simon	one of Jesus' 12 disciples
Potiphar	an Egyptian official who employed Joseph
Rachel	wife of Jacob
Sarai/Sarah	Abraham's wife; went with Abraham when God called him to travel to Canaan
Silas	he spoke about Jesus and travelled with **Paul**
Simon	see Peter
Solomon	David's son; wise, wealthy but stopped obeying God

CHILDREN'S GUIDE TO THE BIBLE

by Robert Willoughby

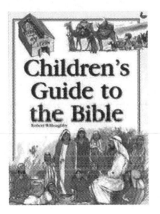

The Bible is like a country waiting to be explored. This book will be your guide. It leads you through the Bible from the beginning to the end and explains God's great plan for the world. Fact boxes, time bars, maps and loads of other information.

£6.99

BIBLE ALIVE

by Penny Boshoff

A fun look at the geography of the Bible. Using photographs, illustrations and maps, the Bible is brought to life as you explore the route maps through the Bible

£7.99

THE STRONG TOWER

by Robert Harrison and Roger Langton

Twelve retold stories about children in the Bible who faced difficult times. Their experiences reflect many of the same situations children face today. Beautifully illustrated!

£7.99

For more details of all these books contact **www.scriptureunion.org.uk**

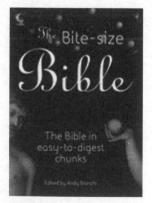

THE BITE-SIZE BIBLE

The story of the Bible in easy-to-digest chunks. A bigger version of *Into the Bible*, with over 200 extracts, *The Bite-size Bible* is a taster to give people the opportunity to read the real Bible text without having to choose where to start!

£9.99

For more details contact **www.harpercollins.co.uk**

Prices correct at the time of printing.